SUBMISSIVE Christian

HUMILITY AND MEEKNESS IN FIVE KEY RELATIONSHIPS

ROBERT E. PICIRILLI

randall house

Table of Contents

Preface

This book makes a case for something that will probably be regarded as counter-cultural. Indeed, submissiveness may even be counter to the culture in our churches! I am confident, however, that it is not counter to biblical teaching. Just about everything in this book comes from the Bible.

"Well, yes," you're going to say, "the Bible *does* recommend humility and meekness as virtues. It *does* teach Christians to submit in certain situations. But, like 'turning the other cheek,' submissiveness isn't very practical and the need for it doesn't arise all that often." If that represents how you feel about the subject, I hope you're going to be surprised. The biblical picture of Christ-followers as submissive in all their relationships is pervasive, and today's church—or any day's church—needs this teaching.

Humility, meekness, and subjection are words that belong in the category of "the fruit of the Spirit." Galatians 5:22-23 (which includes one of these words) isn't meant to be a complete list of the graces that characterize the maturing believer. Spiritual fruit describes the nature of Christian character and includes anything that names what a Christian ought to be and demonstrate in a way that is visible to others.

I'm persuaded that the development of these ripening qualities is at the heart of what it means for a believer in Christ to grow. There is no such thing as a mature Christian who does not grow

1

in love, joy, peace, patience, and self-discipline, to name a few of many possible graces—and humility, meekness, and submissiveness.

That these are within the "fruit of the Spirit" means that the Spirit of God is at work to produce them and bring them to maturity in us in practical ways where we carry on our daily conduct and speech. He uses God's Word, others, and the daily circumstances of our lives to help us in this project.

Even so, this is a joint project. That these are the Spirit's fruit does not mean we have no responsibility. The first fruit in the list is *love*. And yet, over and over, the Bible lays on us the responsibility to love. The same could be said for all the graces in the list and any others—there are many—in the New Testament. One grace in the list of the fruit is *joy*, and yet Paul tells us, "Hey, you there: *rejoice* in the Lord" (Philippians 4:4, free rendering). So we have to shoulder the responsibility; one way to cooperate with the Spirit is to be obedient as far as we already know how.

In this "project" I've referred to, the goal of the Spirit of God is *to change the very kinds of persons we are*. Sometimes I hear a Christian excuse herself or himself by saying something like, "Well that's just the way I am and you'll just have to allow for it." This may be a valid response for new Christians, but God wants to change the kinds of persons we are. And one way He is at work is to make us humble and meek: submissive, in other words.

So what can we do to help? What *should* we do? To oversimplify a little, we should form as complete a picture as we can of what the Bible means by submissiveness, develop that picture in practical terms that fit life on the street where we live, and then set about to put what we learn into practice. I mean for this book to help you, the reader, do this.

This is the project that will enable the Spirit to produce this fruit in us, and to help us grow toward spiritual maturity. The world we inhabit ought to see this kind of character in us and take note that we have been with Jesus.

Chapter 1

Humility

(A Word Study)

Humility and meekness are the two key words necessary for understanding what the Bible teaches about Christian submissiveness. This chapter is a word study intended to help us grasp the biblical meaning of the first one, humility.

I've heard it said that humility is an elusive virtue, that the moment you think you've achieved it, you lose it. There may be some truth in that, but I feel sure the Lord intends for us to be consciously and intentionally humble.

Yet I wonder if anyone really wants to be humble. Humility isn't all that highly regarded in our culture. Many people think that to be humble means to let everybody walk all over you, and who wants that?! Our culture, instead, teaches us to be independent and assertive, to stand up for our rights. Some years ago, there was even a book—I don't know whether it was a bestseller—entitled *Winning through Intimidation*.[1] I didn't read it, but I would guess that the author didn't push humility.

---

[1] Robert J. Ringer, *Winning through Intimidation* (Ballantine Books, 1974).

When people think of a humble person, they probably picture some cartoon character like Ziggy. I remember one that was popular in my youth. He was named Caspar Milquetoast, and the newspaper comic that featured him—one of those single-panel ones, usually—was named "The Timid Soul." Caspar's creator, H. T. Webster, described him as the man who speaks softly and gets hit with a big stick. One panel showed him standing in front of a "Watch This Space" sign, saying, "Well, if something doesn't happen soon, I'm going to have to leave." Caspar was a fall guy, a wimp.

Is that what humility is like? I don't think so. Jesus didn't think so. He recommended humility as one characteristic of a strong and godly person. The Bible provides plenty of evidence for that.

Survey of the Scriptural Usage of the Word

The main Greek noun translated *humility* (in the New Testament) is one of a family of several words in that language. Only the main noun and the adjective appear in the New Testament, a total of eight times:

- Noun: *humility (tapeinophrosunē)*—Acts 20:19; Ephesians 4:2; Philippians 2:3; Colossians 2:18, 23; 3:12; 1 Peter 5:5.
- Adjective: *humble (tapeinophrōn)*—1 Peter 3:8 (in some manuscripts).

Here follow preliminary observations about each of these; the underlined words (in the King James Version quoted) translate the Greek word meaning *humility* or *humble*.

1. Acts 20:19: "Serving the Lord with all <u>humility of mind</u> (ESV: humility), and with many tears, and temptations which befell me by the lying in wait of the Jews."

This is part of Paul's farewell address to the Ephesian elders, near the end of his third missionary journey. He began by reminding them of the personal example he had set for them, in the way he had lived among them (verse 18). Verse 19 is the very first thing he said about that, a characteristic that no doubt summarized everything else about his ministry there: namely, he served the Lord with all or utmost *humility*.

2. Ephesians 4:2: "With all <u>lowliness</u> (ESV: humility) and meekness, with longsuffering, forbearing one another in love." Paul is urging his readers to walk in a way that is worthy of the Lord who called them to Himself, and the very first characteristic is lowliness or humility.

3. Philippians 2:3: "Let nothing be done through strife or vainglory; but in <u>lowliness of mind</u> (ESV: humility) let each esteem other better than themselves." Paul urges his readers to fulfill his joy (verse 2) and follow the example of Jesus (verse 5) in humility.

4. 5. Colossians 2:18a, 23a: "Let no man beguile you of your reward in a voluntary <u>humility</u> (NKJV: *false* humility; ESV: asceticism) and worshipping of angels" (18a). "Which things have indeed a shew of wisdom in will worship and <u>humility</u>" (NKJV: *false* humility; ESV: asceticism) (23a). This is a manifestation of humility that Paul is condemning, not commending; it represents a misdirected humbling or lowering of oneself that is not biblical.

6. Colossians 3:12: "Put on therefore, as the elect of God, holy and beloved, bowels of mercies, kindness, <u>humbleness of mind</u>

(ESV: humility), meekness, longsuffering." In this section Paul emphasizes the difference between "the old man" (one's way of life before conversion) and "the new man" (the way of life of a converted person), appealing for humility.

7. 1 Peter 5:5b: "All of you be subject one to another, and be clothed with humility (ESV: humility).

8. 1 Peter 3:8 has the adjective (not in all manuscripts; the text translated by the King James has a different word, *courteous*). ESV: "Finally, all of you have unity of mind, sympathy, brotherly love, a tender heart, and a humble mind."

As one can see, this Greek root appears only in the writings of Paul (and only in his prison epistles), once in Acts quoting Paul, and in a letter from Peter—who shows acquaintance with Paul (cf. 2 Peter 3:15). That fact doesn't mean that it was an exclusively Pauline word, of course, but Paul apparently was accustomed to use it as an important quality for a Christian to develop.

What Does the Word Mean?

The etymology of the Greek word may suggest its meaning.[2] It is a compound with two parts. The first (*tapeino-*) means *lowly* and the second (*phron-*) means the *mind* or *thought*. Thus the word suggests being lowly-minded or thinking oneself to be lowly. True, words mean what they are used to mean, and in this case, the idea of lowliness or humility of mind is right.

---

[2] Linguists do not think highly of determining the meaning of a word primarily by its etymology; but etymology should not be ignored entirely.

The King James translators used five different English expressions for this word in translation, as seen above: *humility of mind, lowliness of mind, humbleness of mind, lowliness,* and *humility.* The ESV used *humility* for all of them except for the misguided humility referred to in Colossians 2:18, 23.

Interestingly, of the two parts of the word just defined, the first part, meaning *lowly,* can be used by itself at times, in the New Testament, to mean about the same thing as the compound word treated above. That root (*tapeino-*) occurs as a noun and as a verb and has a broad range of meanings, all of them reflecting the idea of *low*-ness. Thus it can refer to a low place spatially, socially, or emotionally; or to lowliness in a negative sense (as in humiliation or abasement) or in a good sense (humility). Among the helpful verses that use the simple word in a good sense to mean humility are:

Matthew 11:29 ("lowly in heart");

Matthew 18:4; 23:12; Luke 14:11; 18:14 ("humble himself");

James 4:6; 1 Peter 5:5 ("the humble");

James 4:10; 1 Peter 5:6 ("humble yourselves").

Other Words Associated With Humility

It is often helpful, in fleshing out the meaning of a word, to take note of other words and expressions closely associated with it in context. Here are some of the words that are helpful as complements to humility

Meekness is linked with humility in Ephesians 4:2, Colossians 3:12, and Matthew 11:29. Since I am going to devote the next chapter to meekness, I will say nothing more about this word now. But be sure of this: understanding meekness requires understanding humility—and vice versa.

In Acts 20:19, Paul closely associates *tears* with humility, especially tears involved in trials brought on him by his fellow Jews that were hostile to the gospel he preached. The implication is that his humility in serving the Lord led to his submissive acceptance of those trials and the tears involved.

In Ephesians 4:2 and Colossians 3:12, *longsuffering* (or *patience*) and *forbearance* are side by side with humility and meekness. People who think humbly of themselves will naturally be more tolerant and patient in their dealings with others.

Colossians 3:12 also names being *merciful* (or *compassionate*), *kind*, and *forgiving* as likely companions of humility—for the same reason.

If being humble is in 1 Peter 3:8, then it is closely linked to a spirit of *unity*, *compassion* (or *sympathy*), *brotherly love*, and *tender-heartedness* (or *showing pity*).

Words That Are in Contrast With Humility

Among the words that stand in contrast to humility, thus helping flesh out its meaning, are the following.

Strife (or *rivalry*) and v*ainglory* (or *conceit*) stand opposite to humility in Philippians 2:3.

In Matthew 23:12, Luke 14:11, and Luke 18:14 to humble oneself is the opposite of *exalting oneself.*

James 4:6 and 1 Peter 5:5 both quote that God resists the *proud* but gives grace to the humble.

Humility, then, according to all these contrasts, is the opposite of pride.

Expressions That Clarify the Meaning of Humility

In several of the passages I have cited there is a phrase or clause attached that serves to expose the practical meaning of humility. These get close to defining the word, but primarily they indicate essential implications. (Quotations are from the King James version again.)

Matthew 11:29: "Take my yoke upon you, and learn of me; for I am meek and lowly in heart." Submission to the "yoke" of Jesus is required for humility. A yoke, by definition, is a harness for service. Humility and service go together essentially.

Acts 20:19: "Serving the Lord with all (or utmost) humility." This makes essentially the same point. Service—and this is the word for bond-service or slavery—is necessarily implied in humility.

James 4:6-7: "[God] giveth grace unto the humble. Submit yourselves therefore to God."

First Peter 5:6: "Humble yourselves therefore under the mighty hand of God." These two passages certainly include the idea of subjection to God in serving Him, but their primary lesson is more pointed. Those who are truly humble will accept and submit to God's dealings with them.

Philippians 2:3: "In humility let each esteem other better than themselves." Those who think highly of themselves are not able to do this; they must always put themselves first. Verse 4, in effect, expresses yet one more way humility shows itself: namely, by focusing on the needs of others rather than selfish concerns. Humility, by definition, will express itself in this way. Paul immediately cites Jesus as the prime example for us to emulate in this. (I will explore Philippians 2:3-11 later.)

First Peter 5:5: "Likewise, ye younger, submit yourselves unto the elder. Yea, all of you be subject one to another, and be clothed with humility." Humility, by definition, involves not only subjection (or submission) to God but also to others, for service, in the body of Christ.

Some Concluding Observations About Humility

This chapter serves primarily to survey the biblical usage of the word *humility*. The data gleaned provides helpful suggestions toward understanding what the Bible means by this beautiful word. We are not finished, of course. The entire book will develop the subject more fully and practically. Meanwhile, some things already seem clear enough—and tantalizing.

In the ancient Greek and Roman culture, even more than in ours, humility was not necessarily regarded as a virtue. To think of oneself as lowly seemed demeaning. A humble person was likely to be servile, they thought, and sure to be stepped on. In that culture, a greater value was placed on being assertive. It is no less than amazing that Christianity was able to give this lowly quality a positive value. Only a radically different way of thinking about spiritual things was able to bring this about.

Indeed, it was the Christians who apparently invented the compound word for humility that has been discussed here: "No Greek writer employed it before the Christian era, nor, apart from the influence of Christian writers, after."[3]

Humility, in the Bible, is to regard oneself as lowly. I still appreciate the words of R. C. Trench, which I first encountered some sixty-five years ago, in defining humility (borrowing from St. Bernard) as "the esteeming of ourselves as small, inasmuch as we are so; the thinking truly, and because truly, therefore lowlily, of ourselves."[4] Humility is *not* thinking of ourselves as lowly even though we know we are more than that, it is thinking of ourselves as lowly because we really are.

Humility points in two directions. First, we think ourselves lowly before God. Many of the verses I have cited, above, speak directly to this. It leads to submission and service, to a willing acceptance of His providential hand in our lives and of His lordship over us.

Second, we think ourselves lowly in relationship to others, especially—but not only—to those with us in the household of faith. Many of the verses I have cited, above, focus on this. Again, this leads to submission—mutual subjection in the church—and service. When we are humble, not thinking highly of ourselves (cf. Romans 12:3), we can easily obey Paul's instruction in Philippians

---

[3] Richard Chenevix Trench, *Synonyms of the New Testament* (Grand Rapids: Eerdmans, 1958) 148.

[4] Trench, *Synonyms* 150.

2:3-5, counting the needs of others more important than our own and in that way exercising the mind that was in Christ Jesus.

This only serves to get us started.

Questions and suggestions for thought or discussion

- Why is it hard to be humble?
- What is it about being humble that seems distasteful?
- In what sort of situations is it most difficult to exercise humility?
- What kinds of attitudes and behavior show the *lack* of humility?
- What qualities are the opposite of humility?
- Can a person be humble and still stand for what's right? How?
- Make a written or mental list of three different situations you often face where humility is needed and describe how humility should be demonstrated in those situations.
- Think of someone whom you would characterize as humble. Identify things about that person's demeanor or actions that you believe demonstrate her or his humility.
- Think of some specific things you want to change, in order to be more spiritually mature in humility, and ask the Lord to help you make those changes.

Chapter 2

Meekness

(A Word Study)

Some words just seem to go together: like salt and pepper, or pen and ink, or even apple pie and ice cream!

Humility and meekness go together. As I said in the previous chapter, to understand one requires understanding the other. Each is essential to the other. You can't have one of these qualities without the other. The two words are like looking at the same virtue from two different perspectives.

Put the two—humility and meekness—together and you have submissiveness.

Again, then, we need to survey the New Testament to see how it uses the word and what meekness means in practical terms.

Survey of the New Testament Usage of *Meekness*

Like the Greek word for humility, the one for this virtue occurs in the New Testament as both a noun, *meekness* (*prautēs*), and an adjective, *meek* (*praus*). Together, they appear fifteen times.

- *Meekness*: 1 Corinthians 4:21; 2 Corinthians 10:1; Galatians 5:23, 6:1; Ephesians 4:2; Colossians 3:12; 2 Timothy 2:25; Titus 3:2; James 1:21, 3:13; 1 Peter 3:15-16.
- *Meek*: Matthew 5:5, 11:29, 21:5; 1 Peter 3:4.

Here are some brief, preliminary observations about these verses, citing the King James Version (and underlining the word in the English translation).

1. Matthew 5:5: "Blessed are the <u>meek</u>, for they shall inherit the earth." Other than using the word itself, this context (the Beatitudes) offers no additional insight into its meaning.

2. Matthew 11:29: "Take my yoke upon you, and learn of me; for I am <u>meek</u> and lowly in heart; and ye shall find rest unto your souls." As already noted, meekness is linked with lowliness (humility) and is a characteristic of Jesus Himself.

3. Matthew 21:5b: "Thy King cometh unto thee, <u>meek</u>, and sitting upon an ass, and a colt the foal of an ass." This quotation (from Zechariah 9:9) is applied to Jesus at the time of his triumphal entry into Jerusalem. That he rode on a donkey (instead, say, of a prancing stallion) represented his coming in peace—and so in meekness.

4. 1 Corinthians 4:21b: "Shall I come to you with a rod, or in love, and in the spirit of <u>meekness</u>?" Paul, recognizing the Corinthians' need for correction of their ways, asks this rhetorical question in anticipation of his next visit among them. Meekness links with love, not with a rod of chastisement.

5. 2 Corinthians 10:1: "Now I Paul myself beseech you by the <u>meekness</u> and gentleness of Christ, who in presence am base

among you, but being absent am bold toward you." Paul was apparently speaking to some in Corinth who resisted his leadership and criticized him as being "base" while present with them but "bold" while he was away and writing letters. The word for "base" is the same as *lowly* or *humble* (the previous chapter). Thus again meekness is associated with humility. It is also linked to "gentleness," and Paul affirms that Christ had both of these qualities.

6. Galatians 5:22-23: "The fruit of the Spirit is … <u>meekness</u>." In this famous list—of the fruit of the Spirit, in contrast to the works of the flesh—meekness is linked to seven other beautiful Christian virtues, especially (it would seem) to peace, longsuffering, and gentleness.

7. Galatians 6:1: "Brethren, if a man be overtaken in a fault, ye which are spiritual, restore such an one in the spirit of <u>meekness</u>, considering thyself, lest thou also be tempted." Meekness is a mark of being spiritually minded, and it is required for those who would restore believers who have fallen into sin.

8. Ephesians 4:2: "With all lowliness and <u>meekness</u>, with longsuffering, forbearing one another in love." Again, meekness is linked with humility (lowliness) and manifests itself in patience and tolerance for fellow believers.

9. Colossians 3:12: "Put on therefore, as the elect of God, holy and beloved, bowels of mercies, kindness, humbleness of mind, <u>meekness</u>, longsuffering, forbearing one another, and forgiving one another." This has been discussed in the previous chapter and links meekness directly with humility once again.

10. 2 Timothy 2:24-25a: "And the servant of the Lord must not strive, but be gentle unto all men, apt to teach, patient, in <u>meek-</u>

ness instructing those that oppose themselves." Paul is teaching Timothy his leadership duties, which will include instructing and correcting those who are in error. Even so, that must be done in meekness, and this quality is linked with gentleness and patience; it is the opposite of causing strife.

11. Titus 3:1-2: "Put them in mind to be subject to principalities and powers, to obey magistrates ... to be no brawlers, but gentle, shewing all meekness unto all men." Paul instructs Titus to teach this manner of life to the believers under his influence. The verses show several ways meekness will be manifested toward others; it is to be *demonstrated* in observable conduct ("showing"), and not just to fellow believers but to unbelievers as well.

12. James 1:21b: "Receive with meekness the engrafted word, which is able to save your souls." Meekness is required in accepting and submitting to the word of God as the saving and guiding force in one's life.

13. James 3:13b: "Let him [the one wise and knowledgeable] shew out of a good conversation (ESV: conduct) his works with meekness of wisdom." In James, wisdom is practical, having a heart for and knowing how to live by the values that please God. That, too, requires meekness.

14. 1 Peter 3:4: "Let [the adornment of Christian wives] ... be ... the ornament of a meek and quiet spirit, which is in the sight of God of great price." As in James, meekness is highly practical, but it characterizes—along with quietness—the *spirit* of godly wives, including those who want to influence their unbelieving husbands for God.

15. 1 Peter 3:15 (16 in some verse divisions): "Be ready always to give an answer to every man that asketh you a reason of the hope that is in you with <u>meekness</u> and fear." Meekness will characterize Christians in their response to people who ask them—perhaps critically or accusingly—the grounds of their hope in Christ.

Question: Is *Meekness* the Best Translation of the Word?

As the survey above shows, the King James Version always uses *meek* (adjective) and *meekness* (noun) for this pair of Greek words. In recent years, however, interpreters and translators have been more inclined to think that some other English word is more accurate than *meekness*. The words more likely to be chosen are *gentle* and *gentleness*.

The English Standard Version (ESV) is a good example, using *gentle/gentleness* in nine of the fifteen places just referenced. Interestingly, it uses *meek/meekness* in Matthew 5:5, 2 Corinthians 10:1, Colossians 3:12, and in James 1:21; 3:13; and *humble* in Matthew 21:5. I tried to discern some reason the ESV translators thought *meekness* and *gentleness* were better fits in the places where they used them, but I could not.

A standard Greek lexicon gives the meanings of the Greek adjective as *gentle, humble, considerate, meek,* and *unassuming*; and the Greek noun as *gentleness, humility, courtesy, considerateness, meekness.*[5] The Louw and Nida lexicon gives *gentleness, meekness, mildness.*[6]

I am not entirely sure why many prefer *gentleness* over *meekness.* Perhaps they think *meekness* isn't properly and positively viewed in our culture. If that is the reason, I am likewise unsure that this is a good motive. It may well be that the Bible intends a word that is not highly regarded in our culture.

I heard or read, somewhere, that the gentleness indicated by this Greek word is like that of a horse that, previously unridden, has been "gentled." I tend to think that meaning has the right idea. My problem with *gentle(ness)* as a translation, however, is that I think most people use it as the opposite of *rough(ness)* or *harsh(ness)*, and I'm not convinced that this is the basic idea in the word. I don't doubt that handling something gently, rather than roughly, can be an element in the meaning of meekness, but I doubt that the primary idea is the opposite of roughness or harshness.

Indeed, then, my inclination is not to abandon the term *meekness.* But if some other English wording is needed to express the primary meaning, I would suggest *submissive* and *submissiveness.* They reflect, as does the Greek pair, both the inner attitude involved and the way one handles situations or deals with others as a result of that attitude. For that matter, the Greek words translated

---

[5] William F. Arndt and F. Wilbur Gingrich, *A Greek-English Lexicon of the New Testament and Other Early Christian Literature* (Chicago: University of Chicago Press, 1957, 1974) 705.

[6] Johannes P. Louw and Eugene A. Nida, *Greek-English Lexicon of the New Testament Based on Semantic Domains,* 2nd ed., vol. I (New York: United Bible Societies, 1988, 1989) 749.

humility (chapter 1) and *meekness* are synonyms and can, at times, be used interchangeably. So are the English words.

Trench's observations are still pertinent, defining the word as "an inwrought grace of the soul; and the exercises of it are first and chiefly towards God.... It is that temper of spirit in which we accept his dealings with us as good, and therefore without disputing or resisting."[7]

Words Closely Associated With Meekness

The meaning of this word, however, is not to be arrived at by merely deciding what English word to use in translation. We must flesh out the meaning, conceptually, more fully than that.[8] One thing helpful in doing this is to take note of the other words with which it is linked. That helps us form a fuller concept of the "meaning" of the word.

First, the most important companion of meekness is humility, as noted already. In Matthew 11:29, Jesus Himself is *meek* and *lowly* (*humble*) in heart. Ephesians 4:2 and Colossians 3:12 both closely link humility and meekness. (More about this later in this chapter.) Even in 2 Corinthians 10:1, Paul's rivals spoke of him as *base*, which is the same word as *lowly* or *humble*, and Paul answers by referring to himself as having the meekness of Christ.

In 1 Corinthians 4:21, Paul associates meekness with *love*. In 2 Corinthians 10:1, he speaks of the meekness and *gentleness* of

---

[7] Trench, *Synonyms* 152.

[8] This is the reason contemporary linguists often speak of words used in translation as *glosses*, distinguishing them from full definitions.

Christ. This last word translates yet another Greek word (*epieikeia*), a close synonym of humility and meekness which the Arndt and Gingrich lexicon says means *clemency, gentleness, graciousness.* Louw and Nida define it as "the quality of gracious forbearing," so to be translated by words like gentleness, graciousness, or forbearing.[9] Trench offers that *gentleness* may be the best translation of this third word, but he hastens to add that even this translation misses the element of equity and fairness that is strongly attached to the word and fails to convey the idea of foregoing one's rights for the sake of others.[10] This same word is again associated with meekness in Titus 3:1-2, where the focus of the instruction is on being in subjection to others. I will devote a chapter, later, to the important relationship between submissiveness and appropriate subjection.

Meekness is also, like humility, linked to *quietness* (1 Peter 3:4). In the same context (1 Peter 3:15-16, it is linked with *fear.* I will devote a chapter to Peter's treatment of submissiveness as fear.

These attractive words that keep company with meekness help us understand the nature of this important virtue.

Words in Contrast With Meekness

Getting a more complete understanding of meekness also results from taking note of the characteristics that are in contrast to it. These include a *rod* of discipline or chastisement (1 Corinthians

---

[9] Louw and Nida, *Lexicon* 749.
[10] Trench, *Synonyms* 157.

4:21), *striving* (2 Timothy 2:24-25), and *brawling* (or *quarreling*; Titus 3:1-2).

Concluding Observations About Humility and Meekness

I think Trench is correct in his understanding of the relationship between these two great Christian virtues.[11] They are synonyms and may at times be interchangeable, but at times there is a noticeable difference between them, along the following lines.

Humility, at heart, is the way a person sees himself or herself: namely, as lowly—though not as inferior or worthless. It is thus, first, a concept of self, but the awareness involved sees this in relationship to others. Most of all, people who are humble see themselves as lowly before God. And then they see themselves, in comparison to other people, as below or subordinate to them: in other words, in such a way as to place the needs and happiness of others above their own selfish interests.

Meekness, then, grows directly out of humility. It is the way humility expresses itself in attitude and actions toward others, both God and other people. The two virtues are inseparable, in that humility is the essential groundwork on which meekness builds, and meekness is the essential outworking of humility in action and attitude. Because a person sees himself humbly, he meekly relates to God and others.

The rest of this book will be devoted to developing this in greater, biblical detail. For now, it may be enough to say that hu-

---

[11] See Trench, *Synonyms* 148–153.

mility and meekness take the form of *submissiveness* before God and in interpersonal relationships. Among the manifestations of this submissiveness will be subjection, self-sacrifice, and service; it is the opposite of selfishness in any form, whether in self-centeredness, self-preservation, or self-promotion.

We're well on our way to understanding submissiveness in the Christian life, but it is still true that we have just begun.

Questions and suggestions for thought or discussion

- Why do you think people (and translations) prefer words other than *meek/meekness*?

- Is meekness weakness? If not, why not?

- What is the relationship (and difference) between humility and meekness? (Make sure the discussion brings out that humility focuses, first, on one's attitude toward oneself, while meekness is more focused on how a humble person responds to God or, especially, to others.)

- Identify a couple of instances in the Bible where you believe the character was displaying meekness or submissiveness.

- Numbers 12:3 says Moses was the meekest man in the world. In what ways (in the immediate context or the broader biblical narrative) did Moses demonstrate meekness? Name any occasions when you think he did *not* act with meekness.

- Make a list of three (or more) instances during the last few days when you were in a situation that involved responding to someone else's words or actions. Indicate whether you responded with meekness or not—and if you didn't, what you should have done differently.

- Considering that humility + meekness = submissiveness, define how you should respond to God in situations like the following (or think of some other examples on your own):

  — You believe He has "called" you to a different form of service.

  — You believe He has rebuked your conscience for something you did wrong. (You may want to imagine a specific something that you're prone to do.)

- In the same light, define how you should respond to others in situations like the following (or think of some other situations you may face):

  — Your employer (or supervisor) has misunderstood something you said or did and has wrongly disciplined you or rebuked you harshly in front of other employees.

  — Another driver has "cut you off" in traffic.

  — Your pastor or deacons have come to talk with you about some conduct they see as not living up to the standards of the church.

Chapter 3

Submissiveness as Fear in 1 Peter

In the previous two chapters, we've focused on the two essential and complementary ingredients of submissiveness: humility and meekness. This chapter examines yet another word that means practically the same thing as submissiveness. That word is *fear*, and the New Testament document that uses and highlights the word with this meaning is 1 Peter.

Indeed, Peter's first letter has much to say about our theme of submissiveness. This chapter explores the letter from that perspective, focusing on how Peter develops the theme. Submissiveness is important in the letter, and the word appears several times. In part—though not exclusively so—this results from the fact that the Christians in Asia Minor, whom Peter was addressing (1:1), were experiencing trials and could expect to continue to experience them. Peter points these Christians to humility and meekness—to submissiveness, in other words—as a basic Christian virtue. And he calls it *fear*.

Introducing the Theme: 1 Peter 1:17

Peter's instruction here is simple and direct: "Conduct your-selves throughout the time of your stay here in fear." In saying this he represents the Christian life as a *sojourning*: that is, a time one spends living in a country that is not home. This word is some-thing of a synonym for *strangers* (or *pilgrims*) in verse 1, and the two words appear side by side in 2:11. In other words, this world is not a true home for Christians. We live on this earth, temporarily, as foreigners or aliens. Our citizenship is in Heaven (Philippians 3:20).

What ought to characterize our lives here, as citizens of Heav-en, says Peter, is *fear*, a positive quality which has about the same meaning as that wonderful biblical expression "the fear of God," or "godly fear" (Hebrews 12:28). We'll examine, below, the other occurrences of *fear* in 1 Peter, and that will help make the meaning clear. This fear is not the same as being afraid or in terror; that's a negative kind of fear that we'll also take notice of. This *good* fear is respect for the holy, a reverential awe that expresses itself in sub-mission. And such fear is first and essentially Godward but then manifests itself in all relationships, especially toward others.

It may be that a familiar Old Testament story at least partially illustrates the meaning of fear in this positive sense. First Kings 21 recounts how wicked King Ahab, together with his equally wicked wife Jezebel, succeeded in murdering Naboth and seizing his vine-yard to satisfy Ahab's lust. God sent word by Elijah: there would be severe judgment. Verse 27 reports that when Ahab heard the sentence God pronounced, he responded in expressions of grief and—as the King James Version translates—he "went *softly*." I wonder exactly what that implies, but I think it might have been something on the order of what Peter means by passing the time of our stay here in *fear*. The NIV says he "went around *meekly*." And the Lord said to Elijah in response (verse 28): "See how Ahab has *humbled* himself before me?" Most certainly Ahab was chastened, and it showed in his attitude and behavior. That's at least part of what Peter has in mind.

Here in 1:17 Peter puts this instruction in a context. He says, "If you call on the Father, who without partiality judges according to each one's work," then pass your time here in fear. Peter assumes it is true[12] that the readers do in fact invoke God as their Father and as the One before whom they will stand in judgment. Living in godly fear, then, will be the logical result of that relationship and awareness. And then Peter adds another qualifying clause: they can do this because they know that they were redeemed "with the precious blood of Christ" (verse 19). This has set them free from the meaningless life they were living as citizens of this world, trapped in the pattern of life of their earthly fathers.

Applying the Principle: 1 Peter 2:13-17

[13] Therefore submit yourselves to every ordinance of man for the Lord's sake, whether to the king as supreme, [14] or to governors, as to those who are sent by him for the punishment of evildoers and *for the* praise of those who do good. [15] For this is the will of God, that by doing good you may put to silence the ignorance of foolish men—[16]

---

[12] This is called a first class condition in Greek, meaning an *if* clause that is assumed to be true.

as free, yet not using liberty as a cloak for vice, but as bondservants of God. [17] Honor all *people*. Love the brotherhood. Fear God. Honor the king.

Peter leads up to this practical instruction by echoing something he has already said (verse 11): "I beg you as sojourners and pilgrims," reflecting 1:1 and 1:17. Verses 13-17, then, are part of his appeal, explaining how the readers are to conduct themselves in fear during their earthly pilgrimage. These five short verses provide details.

Verse 17 is a pithy summary of a broad application in four commands: Give honor to all, show love to Christian fellow believers, show fear to God, show honor to the king.[13] The last two may consciously reflect Proverbs 24:21. What is clear, now, is that fear (the verb of the noun used in 1:17) is directed to God.

This Godward fear, then, manifests itself in honoring all others, in loving fellow believers, and in honoring the king. Verses 13-16 focus on the last of these, adding detail and expanding it to include not just the king (verse 13b; for them, the Roman Emperor), but also others who govern, at various levels (verses 14-16), as well as the laws and structures they create (verse 13a). Peter develops this command in ways similar to Paul's instruction in Romans 13:1-7. Peter was probably aware of that passage (see 2 Peter 3:15-

---

[13] In the original, the first verb is aorist, the tense that focuses on the act as a whole (thus perhaps "decisive"), while the other three are present, the tense that focuses on action in progress. I attempted to convey this by using *give* and *show*; but this difference need not be overemphasized. It is a matter of perspective, not necessarily of any difference in action. All four should be settled decisions, and all four should be ongoing practice.

16); he focuses on the principles involved in this divinely ordained plan for human government.

Something important appears here: namely, that this fear implies *submission* (verse 13). Specifically, the Christian who in fear honors those who govern, submits to the system of laws they create, and thus to those in authority themselves. Yes, our citizenship is in Heaven, but we must be good citizens here where we sojourn.

God has ordained that we put ourselves in subjection to human authorities. That is what *submit* (*hupotassō*) means: literally, to put oneself under someone or something else. *Submission, subjection, subordination*—either word will do.

When Peter adds, "for the Lord's sake," we see that being in subjection to the laws and structures of human government is grounded in our relationship to Jesus. His authority lies behind that of civil authorities, and in submitting to them we are submitting to Him and pleasing Him.

Verse 16 adds to this: "as bondservants of God." The word *bondservants* is, literally, *slaves*, which further qualifies the submission required. This does not mean *like* servants; it means as the servants we are. And here is a paradox. We are free, as Peter affirms, and yet we voluntarily submit our freedom to the civil structures that govern us.

First Application of the Principle: 1 Peter 2:18-25

Verse 18 provides the injunction: "Servants, be submissive to your masters with all fear, not only to the good and gentle, but also to the harsh." This is the first in a series of applications that will be connected by *likewise* (3:1, 7) and *finally* (3:8). These follow immediately on the heels of verse 17 and are logically linked to it.

The first specific application of living in fear and practicing submissiveness lies in the subjection of servants to their masters. This passage reminds us precisely of, and underscores the authority of, passages like Ephesians 6:5-9 and Colossians 3:22–4:1—except that Peter does not directly address the masters. True, Peter does not use, for *servants*, the word that means bondservants or slaves (*douloi*); instead, he uses the word best translated "household servants" (*oiketai*)—perhaps to emphasize the family relationship. In New Testament times, slaves were considered part of the household or family. Even so, Peter's use of *masters* (*despotai*), as well as his reference to their being beaten (verse 20) apparently indicates that he is thinking of slaves.

Like Paul, Peter is also addressing servants who are *Christians*, and it is important to recognize that the New Testament did not teach them to rebel against their masters and overthrow slavery. Instead, it taught them how to be true Christians regardless of their circumstances. There is a time for Christians to overturn unjust socioeconomic structures, to be sure. So long as Christians are in legal relationships that cannot yet be abolished, however, they are to manifest the submissiveness of humility and meekness. This is part of conducting themselves, throughout the time of their stay here, in *fear* (1:17), and it is part of obeying the injunctions in 2:17.

Verse 18 clarifies that this submission is to *any* masters, whether they are "good and gentle" or "harsh." This was no doubt incorporated in 2:17 as attributing honor to *all* others. Here it involves showing reverence and respect that will be demonstrated in willing obedience, and not being begrudging or resentful in that obedience.

Furthermore, this fear or submissiveness will be maintained even when one is beaten for no good reason. Verse 20 makes clear that there is no special credit that accrues to one who is beaten for good reason and "takes it patiently"; but to take patiently a beating that is undeserved is creditworthy indeed. "Take patiently" (*hupomenō*) is, literally, to bear up under and so to persevere or endure. Peter makes clear that this is part of being submissive, of living in "fear."

Some interpreters are reluctant to take Peter to mean that fear can be directed to anyone other than God Himself. But Peter only makes God the object of fear once, in 2:17; in all his other uses (1:17; 2:18; 3:2, 15), the word is open-ended and embraces others in its purview. It is true, of course, that for a Christian the fear of God lies behind the manifestation of this respectful submissiveness toward others. Here in verse 19, Peter's phrase "because of conscience toward God" intentionally incorporates that idea.

One more thing about this submissiveness, even when servants are mistreated: Jesus serves as our example. Verses 21-24 develop this important motivation. Jesus submitted to the suffering of the cross for the sake of our redemption, and He did so without resentment or retaliation, committing everything about the matter to God.

Whether using the words *humility* and *meekness*, then, or *submissiveness* or *fear*, this is the Christian's calling (verse 21): to be accepting—without resentment or resistance—of the treatment

experienced at the hands of others, even when—*especially* when—
that treatment is undeserved mistreatment.

Second Application of the Principle: 1 Peter 3:1-6

The second practical application Peter makes is summed up
in this: "Wives, likewise be submissive to your own husbands"—
which, like the appeal to servants, reminds us of Paul's instructions
in Ephesians and Colossians. Peter develops the theme somewhat
differently; he consciously views this in the context of the *fear* he
has urged: "when they (the husbands) observe your chaste conduct accompanied by fear" (verse 2).

The husbands to be shown such submissiveness or fear include
those that are unconverted. Indeed, that is Peter's focal point. The
rest of the passage illustrates some of the forms in which this submissive fear will be expressed. These include "chaste conduct"
(verse 2), which refers to a way of life that is pure—from the in-
side out.

Also included is a focus on inner, more than outward, beauty
(verses 3-4), and this will require "a gentle and quiet spirit." Here
gentle is *meek*, one of the key words involved in this study. And
quiet translates a word (*hēsuchios*) that suggests being calm and at
peace—yes, and not creating a disturbance. Such a person manifests a deep-rooted satisfaction of the soul. I am convinced that
this phrase, "a meek and quiet spirit," encapsulates, at its essence,
what Peter means by "in fear."

Peter provides an example from the Old Testament: the wives
of the patriarchs were submissive to their husbands, and in this

they were holy, trusting God, and adorning themselves appropriately. Sarah, specifically, demonstrated her submissiveness in obeying Abraham and calling him lord (apparently reflecting Genesis 18:12).

I will have more to say about wives' submissiveness in a later chapter expounding Ephesians 5. Even so, it is already clear that this is one of the practical relationships in which Christians express submissiveness and conduct themselves in fear.

However, Peter adds a very important qualification at the end of this passage in verse 6: "if you ... are not *afraid* with any terror." I will return to this in treating verse 14, below.

Third Application of the Principle: 1 Peter 3:7

Peter does not have as much to say to husbands as he has said to wives. Nonetheless, he addresses husbands according to the same principle. That he is thinking along the same lines is clear in two ways. First, he introduces the subject with "Likewise," chaining the appeal together with 2:13, 2:18, and 3:1. Second, he uses a word he has introduced in 2:17, *honor*. In the context, Peter is using *honor* to flesh out the implications of the submissiveness he was promoting when he urged his readers to conduct themselves, during the time of their stay here, in fear.

Husbands also, then, manifest this submissiveness in giving honor to their wives. And even though the verse is short, Peter wraps this honor in a description that has several implications. First, this means living together with understanding (or knowledge), and the whole verse clarifies what that understanding involves. Second, the wife is, literally, "the feminine one" (rather than the usual word for wife) and so the "weaker" vessel, probably referring to physical weakness as compared to the stronger male (who is also a "vessel"). Third, the two are equally heirs of the saving grace of eternal life; there is no difference in role in that regard.

In summary, then, the Christian husband—regardless of the temporary difference in roles—likewise manifests submissiveness in assigning to his wife the place of honor. In this sense husbands, too, live "in fear" and subordinate themselves to their wives and their wives' needs. More will be said about this in the discussion of Paul's instruction to husbands in Ephesians and Colossians.

Final, Broader Application of the Principle: 1 Peter 3:8-22

In verse 8, "finally" introduces the last of the series Peter has been developing: the general principle for all in 2:13-17—as applied to household servants in 2:18-25, to wives in 3:1-6, and to husbands in 3:7. The application, now, is for the whole Christian community: "Finally, all of you be of one mind, having compassion for one another; love as brothers, be tenderhearted, be courteous" (1 Peter 3:8).

Though each is broad, these are practical ways for Christians to conduct themselves, during their stay here, in fear (1:17), thus demonstrating the virtue of submissiveness. There are five such ways, in fact. First is *being of one mind*: that is, having unity and harmony of purpose. Second is *showing compassion* for each other as fellow believers; to show compassion is, literally, to "feel with" others. Third is *loving* fellow believers as spiritual brothers and sisters. Fourth is *being tenderhearted*, which means being responsive to the needs of others from deep within; the King James Version's "pitiful" means being full of pity. And fifth is *being courteous—* or *humble*. Some manuscripts have the first word, as in the KJV, which means to be friendly or kindly disposed to others. Some manuscripts have *humble* (or *lowly-minded*), which has been discussed in chapter 1.

These are practical manifestations of the submissiveness indicated by humility and meekness, or by the fear Peter mentions in 1:17. All the characteristics named here grow out of thinking oneself to be lowly—humility, in other words—and then relating meekly to God and others, like Jesus. Believers who have such a disposition will have no trouble being in harmony with others of like mind. They will be quick to show compassion in response to others' pains, to demonstrate self-sacrificing love for fellow Christians (focusing on their needs rather than on themselves, Philippians 2:4). They will find it second nature to be kindly disposed, or humble, in dealing with other human beings.

Without dwelling on the rest of chapter three, a couple of other observations seem appropriate. One is that this kind of submissiveness will *not* retaliate when mistreated. Peter has already made that point with reference to servants (2:18-25) and now he makes it for all his readers (3:9-17). Again he cites the example of Christ Himself, who suffered without resentment, resistance, or retaliation (verse 18).

Especially important is 3:14, which Peter sets in the context of suffering unjustly at the hands of those hostile to Christians. He quotes from Isaiah 8:12-13: "Do not be afraid of their threats, nor be troubled." In other words, when Christians are persecuted by others, they respond in one kind of fear (as in 1:17): that is, in humble and meek submissiveness, foregoing retaliation. But they must not respond in another kind of fear: that is, in being intimidated by their threats so as to be turned aside from faithfulness to God.

The word for *fear* has already been used this way in 3:6, the only two places where it has a negative sense in Peter's letter. Yes, we are to conduct ourselves, during the time of our stay here, in fear (1:17)—fear of God and submissiveness toward others. However, Christians are not under the final dominion of other human beings and must therefore not be afraid of them and what they can do, much less intimidated into disobeying God. Still, when confronted with hostility they are humble and meek—submissive, accepting persecution for Christ's sake (and hearing His "blessing" of them for that, Matthew 5:10-12) and so conducting themselves, rightly, in fear.

A good example of this negative use of *fear* occurs in Hebrews 11 and the "Hall of Fame of Faith." There, the writer says that Moses's parents "were not *afraid* of the king's command" (verse 23) and that Moses himself "forsook Egypt, not *fearing* the wrath of the king" (verse 27). Moses and his parents manifested the good fear that Peter is commending in his letter and often demonstrated that in humility and meekness; but they were *not* afraid in the wrong way, they were not intimidated into surrendering their commitment to God in faith.

Verse 15 seals this discussion. In all circumstances, including when being targets of persecution, Christians are to be ready to answer those who ask them the basis of their hope or confidence; and they are to do this "with meekness and fear." Thus Peter returns to the positive use of *fear* he has been explaining ever since 2:17 and links it to meekness (as explained in chapter 2) to help us understand better what he means by fear. This is Peter's final use of *fear* in the letter and completes his treatment of it as a disposition of reverence and respect toward God that finds expression in one's attitudes and actions toward others. It yields the fruit of humility and meekness and thus manifests itself in submissiveness.

Humility and Submissiveness in 1 Peter 5:5-6

> [5] Likewise you younger people, submit yourselves to *your* elders. Yes, all of *you* be submissive to one another, and be clothed with humility, for
>
> "God resists the proud,
>
> But gives grace to the humble."
> [6] Therefore humble yourselves under the mighty hand of God, that He may exalt you in due time.

Peter returns to the subject of submissiveness to introduce a conclusion to the whole letter. The two verses do two things.

First, Peter specifically calls for the younger believers in the community to be submissive toward the elders. Two questions arise. One question is, what is the implication of the "Likewise"? Probably Peter means in a manner like that of the official elders addressed in the immediately preceding verses, who must be in subjection to the Chief Shepherd, Jesus Christ.

The other question is, who does he mean by "elders"? Older people in general? Or the official "elders" of the church? Some interpreters take one view, some the other. For our purposes here, either will do; what's important for our discussion here is what follows.

Second, then, Peter broadens his appeal to include all who are in the Christian community. All of them are to practice mutual submission (or subjection). In asking for this, Peter matches Paul's injunction in Ephesians 5:21: "submitting to one another in the fear of God"—where also submission and fear are indelibly linked. (This will be discussed again in a later chapter.) It is true that some manuscripts have a shorter wording and simply follow the appeal to the younger by saying, "Yes, all of you be clothed with humility one to another." But the implication is clear that this means mutual submissiveness.

This mutual submissiveness is a manifestation of *humility*. Three times in these short sentences Peter sounds the word *humility* or *humble*, like one who rings a bell to get attention. First (verse 5) is the direct injunction: "Be clothed with humility." This is so linked with being submissive toward each other that this submission is required for Peter's appeal to be obeyed. It is humility, thinking of oneself as lowly, that enables submissiveness or meekness.

Then Peter quotes Scripture (Proverbs 3:34, LXX) to say that God resists the proud but manifests grace to the humble. This has a double impact, showing first that pride (thinking highly of oneself) is the opposite of humility (thinking of oneself as lowly). Then it shows God's relationship to both, resisting the proud and giving grace to those who manifest humility in submissiveness or meekness.

Then Peter exhorts the readers (in essentially the same language as in James 4:10) to humble themselves under the hand of God. They are to think of themselves as lowly and of God as highly exalted. Such a God has absolute authority, and they are to meekly accept His dealings with them. That will be true in all circumstances, the good and the bad, including the persecution that was so much on the minds of Peter's original readers. God will lift them up in His own good time, but that is not the case right now. Verse 7, by the way, is connected; if we humble ourselves under the hand of God, then we can turn all our worries over to Him.

Conclusion

Peter has given us a full treatment of the virtue of submissiveness, which he has linked closely to the words humility and meekness and summarized the whole as *fear*. We are but pilgrims on this earth, and our lives here are to be characterized by the practice of this virtue. All of this is implied in his sweeping appeal in 1:17, "conduct yourselves throughout the time of your stay here in fear."

Questions and suggestions for thought or discussion

- What are some implications of 1 Peter 1:17—"Pass the time of your stay here in fear"—for the way we view and conduct our lives?

- How is Peter, in this epistle, using the word *fear*, and why does he link it so closely with submissiveness?

- Identify some specific ways Christians might apply Peter's words for slaves to employees in today's world.

- If you're married, whether husband or wife, write or name two or three specific ways you should demonstrate submissiveness to your mate. (Then in the coming days put that into action and watch to see if he or she notices!)

- Identify situations in your life where you are interacting with persons who are not Christians. Then ask yourself whether you think they view you as conducting yourself, in your daily life, in "fear." List some ways you may be able to demonstrate submissiveness in your relationships with them.

Chapter 4

Humility, Meekness, and Submissiveness in the Old Testament

ost of this book deals with New Testament material. After all, the New Testament represents the fulfillment of the Old, and the New contains divinely-inspired teaching for Christians in the age of the cross. The New Testament speaks directly to the church and individual believers and provides the principles that ought to shape our lives.

Even so, the Old Testament, although it is often under-appreciated in the church, is an important part of God's revelation of Himself to His people of all ages. In the Old, we find much to identify with. Primarily, the Old spoke to the people of God in a dispensation of spiritual immaturity, under the Mosaic Law as their "child-conductor" (Galatians 3:25). Even so, there is more spiritually mature teaching there than people may think. The lessons may be wrapped in trappings that don't quite fit our circumstances, but kernel principles are there.

Without attempting to be thorough, I thought it would be helpful to provide an overview of how the Old Testament, like the New, speaks to us about humility and meekness, living in the fear of the Lord, and showing ourselves submissive to God and others.

Some Tendencies of Old Testament Teaching on the Subject

Spending some time with an English concordance (to the King James Version) leads to some general observations about the words that are being emphasized in this book. For one thing, the verbs *submit* or *subject* and nouns *submission* or *subjection* occur only a few times, mostly in the context of the military submission of one people to another or in the context of personal slavery. When the Angel of the Lord told Hagar, "Return to your mistress and *submit* yourself under her hand" (Genesis 16:9), that pretty well represents the Old Testament use of this word. It also illustrates the basic nature of submission.

Humility (or the verb and adjective *humble*) and *meekness* occur more often, and the two ideas are not distinguished. By and large, the very same Hebrew words are translated in either way in the KJV; more recent versions usually translate this *humble/humility*, but sometimes *meek/meekness*. As compared to the New Testament, this word does not so often refer to an attitude or spirit within a person. More often, it refers to what we might call *visible* or outward humbling. Sometimes it means outright humiliation, as when a woman is said to be "humbled" by a rapist, for example (see Deuteronomy 22:24, 29). Often, the word refers to persons in what we might call "humble circumstances," as being needy or helpless (see Job 22:29; Psalm 9:12; 10:17). Even these serve to illustrate the basic meaning of humility, in that such people are in a *lowly* condition.

Still, there are numerous instances in the Old Testament when *humility* or *meekness* appear in ways that suggest meanings similar to their use in the New Testament, and the following sections, although they are not exhaustive, serve to expand our understanding of the nature of these virtues in a way that still applies to us.

I should add that *pride*, as the opposite of humility and meekness (submissiveness), occurs many times in the Old Testament. Some of these will come to light in one or more of the following sections.

Kings Who Did or Did Not Humble Themselves Before God

An especially interesting and illustrative section of 2 Chronicles[14], toward the end of the kingdom of Judah, gives pointed teaching about the nature of humility as submissiveness. In the space of five chapters or so, we meet five kings who are evaluated by this very criterion.

---

[14] It is worth noting that one characteristic of the two books of Chronicles, as compared to the two books of Kings, is to devote more attention to the spiritual implications of the narrative.

For Hezekiah see 32:25-26. As hard as it is to believe, even after God had delivered Judah from the Assyrians under Sennacherib (verse 22) and had saved Hezekiah from death and extended his life (verse 24), verse 25 reports that "his heart was lifted up" and God's wrath loomed. Perhaps deliverance had gone to his head. But his pride did not continue; the very next verse reports that he "*humbled* himself for the pride of his heart, he and the inhabitants of Jerusalem, so that the wrath of the Lord did not come upon them in the days of Hezekiah."

The next king was Hezekiah's son Manasseh, taking the throne at age twelve. His wickedness is the subject of 33:1-10, summed up thus: "Manasseh seduced Judah and the inhabitants of Jerusalem to do … evil" (verse 9). The Lord spoke to him, but in his pride he "would not listen" (verse 10; ESV: "paid no attention"). As a result, the Lord brought him personally into captivity; the enemies came, "took Manasseh with hooks," and took him away to Babylon (verse 11). Amazingly, in his humiliation Manasseh "*humbled* himself greatly" before God and prayed to Him. God heard and brought him back to his kingdom (verses 12, 13), and Manasseh came to understand that the Lord is God. Then he attempted—with only partial success—to undo the evil he had wrought (verses 14-17).

Manasseh's son Amon succeeded him to the throne, and little is said about his two-year, failed reign. Except this: "And he did not humble himself before the LORD, as his father Manasseh had humbled himself; but Amon trespassed more and more. Then his servants conspired against him, and killed him in his own house" (33:23-24).

After Amon came his son, good king Josiah, who undertook to restore the pure worship of the Lord. In the midst of his reforms he sent to inquire of Huldah, God's spokeswoman, who responded that judgment was still to come but that it would be suspended until after Josiah's reign was finished. The message to Josiah was this: "'Because your heart was tender and you humbled yourself before God when you heard His words ... I also have heard you,' says the Lord" (34:27).

Josiah was the last of the good kings. In the few years that followed his reign, a succession of Josiah's family members occupied the throne for shorter or longer times, all wicked: Jehoahaz, Eliakim (Jehoiakim), and Jehoiachin. The last was Zedekiah, of whom the Chronicler says, "He also did evil in the sight of the Lord his God, and did not *humble* himself before Jeremiah the prophet, who spoke from the mouth of the Lord" (36:12).

What did this expression, to *humble* oneself before the Lord, mean? Whatever else it might have meant, it included submissiveness. In the circumstances then prevailing, that primarily meant to repent of sin and to worship and obey God alone. As kings, being humble before God meant reigning under God's reign, being in subjection to Him.

Submissiveness is the opposite of pride, of having one's own way and doing one's own thing instead of following God's way and doing God's thing.

For other kings who were evaluated by this same standard, see Rehoboam (2 Chronicles 12:6, 7, 12) and Belshazzar (Daniel 5:22-23).

Humility and Meekness in the Psalms

As a "devotional" book, Psalms speaks often about this quality of character. As noted already, sometimes the word *humble* refers to lowly or helpless circumstances, but many references get close to the humility of heart that the New Testament has much to say about. Here are some especially helpful passages.

- 25:9: "The *humble* He guides in justice, And the *humble* He teaches His way."

- 34:2: "My soul shall make its boast in the Lord; The *humble* shall hear of it and be glad."

- 37:11: "But the *meek* shall inherit the earth, And shall delight themselves in the abundance of peace."

- 45:3-4: "Gird Your sword upon Your thigh, O Mighty One, With your glory and Your majesty. And in your majesty ride prosperously because of truth, *humility*, and righteousness."

- 69:32: "The *humble* shall see this and be glad; And you who seek God, your hearts shall live."

- 147:6: "The Lord lifts up the *humble*; He casts the wicked down to the ground."

- 149:4: "For the Lord takes pleasure in His people; He will beautify the *humble* with salvation."

We learn several things about humility from these psalms: (1) Submissive people are teachable (25:9). (2) They rejoice when God is praised (34:2; 69:32) rather than themselves. (3) They will "inherit" the land (37:11). Psalm 37 equates "the meek" with those "who wait on the Lord" (verse 9), who are "blessed by Him" (verse

21), who are "righteous" (verse 29); and they will inherit rather than the wicked who trust and boast in their riches. (4) The Messiah's kingdom will be built on humility, truth, and righteousness (45:3-4). (5) The humble stand in contrast to the wicked, and even if they are in lowly circumstances now the Lord will lift them up in full deliverance (147:6; 149:4).

Humility Versus Pride in Proverbs

Readers may find surprising just how much Proverbs has to say about the submissive life. Proverbs has a way of making positive teaching clearer by providing contrast with its opposite: a sharpening of focus by comparing negative practices.

After all, two of the most important words in Proverbs are *wisdom* and *fools*, and this book of the Bible draws a dramatic line of distinction between the two, commending one and ridiculing the other. Biblical wisdom is highly practical, teaching how to live in the fear of the Lord. Humility is one of the marks of that wisdom. Pride, on the other hand, is the way of the fool.

Proverbs has a lot to say about humility, and it's all positive. By contrast, everything it says about pride, the opposite of humility, is negative. Consider, for example, 3:34: "He scorns the scornful, But gives grace to the humble"—which is the source of James 4:6 and 1 Peter 5:5. Being scornful or scoffing comes from pride and doesn't lead to grace. God gives grace to those who humble themselves before Him and then meekly reflect that attitude in all their dealings with Him and others.

Consider also some other nuggets of wisdom, like 11:2: "When pride comes, then comes shame; But with the humble is

wisdom." Then there's 16:19: "Better to be of a humble spirit with
the lowly, Than to divide the spoil with the proud." Or 18:12: "Before destruction the heart of a man is haughty, And before hon-
or is humility" (compare 15:33). "Haughty" is another word for
proud. Here, too, is 22:4: "By humility and the fear of the Lord Are
riches and honor and life"—linking humility directly to the fear of
the Lord. As in 15:33, this couplet is entirely positive, expressing
an important truth about the nature of humility in line 1 and the
reward of humility in line 2.

Another proverb that exposes the danger of pride and attaches good promises to humility is 29:23: "A man's pride will bring
him low, But the humble in spirit will retain honor." Again, pride
and humility are opposites and the proverb is ironic; pride leads to
its opposite, lowliness; and lowliness in heart leads to its opposite,
being raised in honor (as in 15:33; 18:12).

If Proverbs makes humility attractive, it likewise exposes the
ugliness of pride. In 6:16-17, for example, one of the "numeric"
proverbs declares that there are six things, yes seven, which the
Lord hates. All seven are abominable to Him: in other words,
things He detests. And the very first one in the list is "a proud
look"—or "haughty eyes" (ESV). Pride isn't popular with the
Lord. See also 16:5.

Consider 8:13: "The fear of the LORD is to hate evil; Pride and
arrogance and the evil way And the perverse mouth I hate." In the
Bible "the fear of the Lord" is respectful, submissive awe of Him,
and those who are characterized in this way will hate—that is, they
will reject and avoid—whatever is evil. As often in Proverbs, "Lady
Wisdom" is speaking here, and she rejects pride and its compan-

ions: arrogant affirmation of one's independence, wicked conduct, and perverse or twisted speech that regards good as evil and evil as good.

In Proverbs 13:10—"By pride comes nothing but strife, But with the well-advised is wisdom"—we learn about yet another companion of pride: namely, a contentious self-assertion that is quarrelsome and leads to discord. In contrast to that is a person who is "well-advised": that is, who is humble enough to recognize and accept good counsel from others. Thus humility equals wisdom.

Not only does the Lord find pride ugly and detestable, He will bring it down to destruction. In 15:25, using contrasting parallelism, the writer states this outright: "The LORD will destroy the house of the proud"; and the opposite: "But He will establish the boundary of the widow." In Israel's culture, widows were by definition lowly and dependent, helpless. The Lord who disdains and destroys the proud will build the humble widow's property and home. Similarly, 16:18 affirms: "Pride goes before destruction, And a haughty spirit before a fall." In the parallelism, this equates pride to a "haughty spirit" or attitude, which is a pretty good definition of pride. Compare 21:24, which shows that a proud or arrogant person is likely to demonstrate his or her sense of superiority in scoffing at or mocking others.

Proverbs 21:4 makes plain that in the eyes of God pride is a sin: "A haughty look, a proud heart, And the plowing of the wicked are sin." Some versions render "the lamp of the wicked" instead of "the plowing of the wicked." Regardless, the point seems to be that whatever one does in life, even normal everyday things, is wicked when it is done in proud independence of God. That's the problem with pride, it rots everything else.

Proverbs, then, provides an excellent, practical contrast between pride and humility. The one is ugly and detestable, the other lovely and appreciated—both by God and by those in tune with God. Pride is linked to arrogance, haughtiness, and contention, and it leads to God's judgment. Humility, by contrast, goes hand in hand with submissiveness, the fear of the Lord, and wisdom; it leads to honor and abundant life and has the approval of God. This matches well what Jesus said in Luke 14:11: "Whoever exalts himself will be humbled, and he who humbles himself will be exalted."

Two Especially Precious Passages

Often the Old Testament rises to the heights of the New. Here are two special passages that appear to regard humility or submissiveness in its full, gospel light. They are worth careful meditation.

Second Chronicles 7:14: "If My people who are called by My name will humble themselves and pray and seek My face, and turn from their wicked ways, then I will hear from heaven and will forgive their sin and heal their land."

It's true, of course, that this was spoken in a specific context. Solomon and the Israelites were dedicating the temple he built, for which his father David had gathered the materials. It was a time of great celebration. Solomon had prayed and fire had come from above and devoured the sacrifice offered. The people had worshipped in heartfelt praise and observed a festival for seven days, after which Solomon had dismissed them to return home in joy.

That night, apparently, the Lord appeared to Solomon to confirm the consecration and restate the covenant relationship between Him and Israel.

Therefore, the words of verse 14, spoken during that confirmation, applied in a specific way to Israel and the blessings or judgment that the Lord might bring on them in the years to follow. Even so, the principles are permanent and apply to the people of God at any place and time.

What we learn about humility or submissiveness that applies to us is that it will be expressed in the three ways indicated here: (1) prayer, (2) seeking God's face, and (3) turning from wickedness. As in the case of Israel, this will especially be true when we have been disobedient and God has initiated chastisement.

More broadly, the verse makes clear that only genuine humility leads to prayer, seeking God's face, and turning from wickedness. Prayer is needing and depending on God. Seeking His face means courting His approval by doing what pleases Him. Turning from wickedness is acknowledging God's authority and law and submitting to it. Proud people, people who are independent and self-asserting, don't do that.

Before anything else, then, true humility is acknowledging oneself as lowly before God and thus meekly submitting to His lordship. That's true for Old and New Testament saints alike.

Micah 6:8: "He has shown you, O man, what is good; And what does the Lord require of you But to do justly, To love mercy, And to walk humbly with your God?"

What a wonderful and powerful statement this is, of what the Lord requires of His people! To be sure, it was spoken to Israel in the days of the Mosaic Law. But it is so basic that its principles are timeless.

In context, the Lord had filed His complaint against backsliding Israel, reminded them of His deliverance of them from Egyptian bondage, and called on them to remember. Micah responded with a question: *How* can he approach God? Will the sacrifices avail? Verse 8 is the answer. What God expects from His people is to "walk humbly," to see themselves as lowly, before God and so to submit to His government of their lives. In a manner of speaking, to do that isn't all that complicated; it will be accomplished by acting and maintaining justice in their relationships with others and by demonstrating to others the mercy that God has shown them.

What's clear in this is that humbling oneself before God entails being just and merciful toward others. To do that is to complement humility with meekness and so to demonstrate submissiveness. I suspect Peter would have accepted this as one definition of "passing the time of your stay here in fear."

Proud people don't push themselves to uphold justice and show mercy. Only those who see themselves as lowly, and their lowliness as being before God, will care about such things.

Conclusion

No doubt other Old Testament passages shed light on the meaning of humility, meekness, and submissiveness. In a subsequent chapter, I will use Moses as an example of such a man. As indicated there, Numbers 12:4 makes the marvelous claim that he was the meekest or humblest man to walk the earth, at least in his time. And, though the word is not applied to Joseph, surely he too provided an excellent example of humbling oneself before God. Likewise, the kings who did and did not humble themselves before God serve as positive and negative examples.

The Old Testament, then, tends to support the New Testament teaching about submissiveness. It is especially focused on sharpening the contrast between humility and pride, the first of the "seven deadly sins." It confirms what we have learned: namely, that humility and meekness grow on the same tree and express themselves in submissiveness before God and toward others.

Questions and suggestions for thought or discussion

- In Isaiah 66:2 the Lord says, "This is the one to whom I will look: he who is humble (NKJV "poor") and contrite in spirit and trembles at my word" (ESV). What does this teach us about humility? What will it mean to "tremble" at God's Word?

- Can you think of any situations in the lives of any kings of Israel or Judah that illustrate humility or the lack of it? How? (If these are too slow in coming, read 1 Kings 21:27-29 and discuss how Ahab's newfound humility manifested itself.

- Read Psalm 25:9 and make written or mental notes identifying what it reveals about humility and how you can apply this teaching in *your* life.

- Do the same for 2 Kings 22:18-20 (read and compare 2 Chronicles 34:23-28) and what is said about good king Josiah and humility. How may we manifest the same kind of humility? What does a "tender heart" have to do with humbling oneself before God?

Chapter 5

The Example of Jesus

Surely we are justified in finding the prime example for our submissiveness in the attitude and actions of our Lord Himself, Jesus Christ. As I intend to show in this chapter, several passages serve to provide us with sure grounds for regarding Jesus as an example in all aspects of the Christian life. Indeed, it is the example of Jesus by which we measure our own spirituality—and being submissive is one mark of being spiritual.

Have you ever been in a home where there were marks made on a door frame or wall, with another mark higher up? The higher mark indicated the father's height when this "record" started, while the several marks at different places down lower represented the height of the son at different ages, measured in comparison with the father. Well, Ephesians 4:11-16 suggests something like that for our spiritual growth. Paul is appealing for the edification, the building up, of the body of Christ, with the goal being "till we all come … to a perfect man" (verse 13). *Perfect* (*teleios*) means complete, having reached the end or goal for which one is designed, and the next phrase provides the standard that identifies the goal: namely, "to the measure of the stature of the fullness of Christ."

Jesus Christ was the perfect embodiment of what God designed a human being to be. We can measure ourselves by Him, as He is revealed in the New Testament. He manifested mature and ideal submissiveness, for example, and by examining closely how He did this we can gain guidelines for ourselves.

Matthew 11:29-30

Here is the text for our treatment of this subject in this chapter, in Jesus' own words: "Take my yoke upon you and learn from Me, for I am gentle and lowly in heart, and you will find rest for your souls. For My yoke is easy and My burden is light." I have already explained that *gentle*, here, is the same word that means *meek*—as defined in chapter 2. *Lowly* means *humble*, as seen in chapter 1. The two words in combination refer both to what one is deep within the inner person, humble or lowly-minded in the heart, and to how one manifests that spirit in interacting meekly with God and other human beings. This is precisely what submissiveness means.

Jesus Himself bears witness that He was and is the very example of submissiveness, so much so that we can take on ourselves the same yoke He wears and learn from Him what we ought to be. This is a powerful and gracious invitation.

Significantly, He invites us to wear a *yoke*, which is a piece of gear that enables one to harness a work animal for a particular task, like pulling a wagon or a plow. The yoke represents service, and only submissive people willingly serve.

But what did Jesus mean by *His* yoke? Is this the yoke He Himself wore? Or the yoke He puts on us? Or the yoke that we wear *with* Him, like one that harnesses two oxen together? These are different, of course, but I'm inclined to think they all lead to the same result: a yoke is a harness for service. No doubt Jesus Himself wore a yoke of service, and He wants us to take that same yoke for our service to Him.

So just how did Jesus demonstrate this submissiveness for us to emulate?

Philippians 2:3-11

This well-known passage describes the most important way Jesus Christ, as the Second Person of the Godhead, humbled Himself as a human being. For our purposes here, the best way to understand this passage is in terms of three major understandings; the reader needs to have the passage open to consult as he or she reads the following analysis.

First, Paul expresses the status of this Second Person of the Godhead *before* the incarnation, in two defining statements (verse 6).

1. He was "in the form of God." The *form* (*morphē*) of His existence was the form or mode in which God exists eternally. In other words, He was God—as John 1:1 indicates.

2. He did not count His equality with God as "robbery." Some interpreters take this to mean that He did not count this equality,

which He enjoyed, as something to be clutched but instead willingly gave it up. More likely, it means He did not consider His equality with God as something wrongly-obtained but as His by right. Either way, the line affirms that He had equality with God in His pre-incarnate state of being.

Second, Paul identifies the action this Person took in actively becoming incarnate, again in two clauses stated as His doing (verses 7-8).

1. He "made Himself of no reputation." Literally, this reads, "He *emptied* Himself," a statement that has engendered much discussion among interpreters of Scripture. Some ask the question, Emptied Himself *of* what? Answers vary. I am satisfied that this is not a question to ask. Instead, the words mean precisely what they say: He emptied *self*.[15] In other words, He ignored any possible selfish considerations and willingly submitted to the incarnation and to the humiliation that followed from it. Some translations read "made himself nothing," and that seems to communicate the right idea.

Think what it must have meant for God to become a human being! To do that He surely had to count as nothing all things *selfish*. He denied all claims that *self* might have made on Him.

2. "He humbled Himself." The first clause, just discussed, focuses more on His action in becoming human. This one focuses

---

[15] See Robert E. Picirilli, "He Emptied Himself (Phil. 2:5-11)," *Biblical Viewpoint* 3:1 [April 1969] 23–30. The Greek verb *emptied* is *kenoō* (noun *kenōsis*), and so the passage has come to be known as the *kenosis* passage or as presenting the *kenosis* or *kenotic* teaching.

more on what He did *as* a human, but the two are closely related and show the same willing, deliberate submissiveness. As I have indicated in the previous chapters, humility is seeing oneself as lowly. It expresses what is at the very heart of submissiveness. Jesus counted Himself lowly and emptied Himself of all self-considerations.

Third, Paul describes the state to which this Person—equal with God but denying self— lowered Himself, in three ways (verses 7-8).

1. He took "the form of a bondservant." The word for bondservant (*doulos*) means a slave, an indentured servant who is entirely at his master's disposal and so in one sense has no will or status of his own. He only does what his master directs or permits. This *form* of existence is in direct contrast to the *form* of God.

2. He took on the likeness (*homoiōma*) and fashion (*schēma*) of a man, a human being—which stands in contrast to His being God. Both of these words (like *morphē above*) can mean *form* or *likeness* or *image* or even *appearance*. Apparently Paul meant that the form Jesus took on, as a servant, in every way—in similarity and in every aspect that would be perceived by others—corresponded to that of a human being. The incarnate Jesus was both fully God and fully human, and a bond-servant among humans at that!

By the way, becoming human may not seem very lowly or humbling to us, but one needs only to consider what that would mean for Him who was truly God forever.

3. Here now is the climactic assertion about the state to which He descended: "He became (*ginomai*) obedient to the point of

death, even the death of the cross." This represents the very lowest point of Jesus' self-humbling; He submitted to cruel, criminal death.

Paul could have said, as he often did, that this was death for us, bearing our sins (as in 2 Corinthians 5:21, for example). That was certainly a part of the humiliation. Instead, Paul says something even more pointed: "even the death of the cross." We may find it hard to appreciate the force of this since we're very used to the idea of Jesus' crucifixion. But in the culture of His time, crucifixion was so shameful that it was not even to be mentioned in polite company. This method of execution, utilized to its cruelest by the Romans, was designed to cause the most excruciating pain and humiliation.

Jesus, in His eternal deity, condescended to become a human bond-slave, condemned and crucified. The Gospels provide some of the details. He was beaten until stripes on His back opened and bled. A mock crown of thorns was pressed into His scalp. He was taunted and slapped in the face, then laughed at for His inability to come down from the cross. His claims were mockingly thrown in His face. His body was literally nailed to the wood, and finally a spear was thrust into His side, reaching up into His chest cavity. This was a death reserved for the worst criminals.

Yet He did not resist. In humility and meekness—perfect submissiveness—He accepted this death as the expression of His rejection by the very ones He came to save.

Fourth, Paul preaches to us the ethical demand that almost overwhelms us: this willing humiliation that Jesus submitted to is the example we are to follow. Paul begins his appeal in verses 3-5 and returns to it in verse 12.

As grounds for the appeal he says, "Let this mind be in you which was also in Christ Jesus" (verse 5). Used this way, *mind* means attitude, way of thinking. Look at the analysis just given, for verses 6-8, and the *mind* of Jesus isn't difficult to define. Hear Him again as He speaks of Himself: "I am meek and lowly in heart."

The main appeal, on this basis (verses 3-4) is: "Let nothing be done through selfish ambition or conceit, but in *lowliness of mind* [there it is again: *humility*!] let each esteem others better than himself. Let each of you look out not only for his own interests, but also for the interests of others." Submissiveness on Jesus' part, and on the part of any of us, is to deny oneself and do what is needed to serve God and others. Emulating Jesus' *mind* entails emulating His humility and meekness, emptying ourselves, and ministering to the needs of others.

Finally, returning to the appeal after detailing Jesus' example, Paul writes (verse 12): "Work out your own salvation with fear and trembling." We must not take this to mean "work *for* our salvation," but to demonstrate our salvation by its practical outworking in our lives. This demonstration will be observable when we live in "fear and trembling." Paul uses the very same word, *fear* (*phobos*), that Peter used often in 1 Peter, where it is another way of naming submissiveness (see chapter 3). Jesus went to the cross in fear and trembling. That submissiveness should characterize our lives.

1 Peter 2:21-24

We return now to 1 Peter 2:21-24 for another treatment of the example Jesus set for us in submissiveness.

> [21] For to this you were called, because Christ also suffered for us, leaving us an example, that you should follow His steps:
> [22] "Who committed no sin,
>   Nor was deceit found in His mouth";
> [23] who, when He was reviled, did not revile in return; when He suffered, He did not threaten, but committed *Himself* to Him who judges righteously; [24] who Himself bore our sins in His own body on the tree, that we, having died to sins, might live for righteousness—by whose stripes you were healed.

These words arise in a context where submissiveness is the main subject, beginning in 1 Peter 2: 13. I have discussed the passage as a whole in chapter 3. Peter is addressing different groups in the church on this subject, servants in the immediate context. He has just reminded believing servants that there is no honor in suffering for their own failures and taking it patiently. However, they are obligated to take it patiently even when they suffer for no fault of their own (verse 20). That is the life to which they are called (verse 21), and Jesus has left an example for them—and us—in this very thing.

Peter's main point is that Jesus, when maltreated and crucified, offered no resistance. Being abusively reviled, He did not offer any reviling in return. Suffering unjustly at the hands of others, He did not lash out at them with threats. Instead, He committed Himself, and His justice, to His Father in Heaven. Peter consciously reflects Isaiah 53:9 in verse 22 and Isaiah 53:5 in verse 24—and perhaps Isaiah 53:7 in verse 23.

Indeed, Peter might have quoted Isaiah 53:7 of the same Messianic Servant Song: "He was led as a lamb to the slaughter, and as a sheep before its shearers is silent, so He opened not His mouth." Did Jesus suffer from the shock of being identified with our sins, or of sensing the Father's withdrawal from Him? We cannot know such things. We can know, however, that He voluntarily submitted to this without any hint of rebellion. Lambs, of course, cannot voluntarily submit to slaughter or shearing; Jesus did.

Some Other Indications of Jesus' Submissiveness

While the passages above are especially crucial in speaking to us of Jesus' submissiveness as our example, there are other significant indications, in the Gospels, of His humility and meekness.

Consider, for example, Luke 2:51-52, which follows immediately the description of Jesus in the temple precincts at age twelve. He had tarried there when His parents had begun the trek back to Nazareth with other Passover pilgrims, causing them some consternation. When that was over, Luke reports, "He went down with them and came to Nazareth, and was subject to them." *Was subject to* translates the verb (*hupotassō*) that is used often in the New Testament to refer to being in subjection or submission. He "learned obedience" (to borrow the words of Hebrews 5:8) at an early age.

Interestingly, right after he reports this, Luke adds, "And Jesus increased in wisdom and stature, and in favor with God and men" (verse 52). That is the inevitable reward of submissiveness, whether for Jesus or for us, His disciples.

The very next thing we learn about Jesus, after His childhood in subjection to His parents, is that He was "led by the Spirit" into the wilderness to be tempted by Satan (Luke 4:1-2). That was not going to be a pleasant experience, but Jesus submitted, without resistance, to the clear leading of the Holy Spirit. He did not think highly of Himself, that He should be exempt from such testing.

Only John's Gospel provides an account of a special, dramatic portrayal of Jesus' submissiveness in the washing of His disciples' feet (John 13:1-17). I have long thought that there is an intentional connection between this scene and the underlying truth of Philippians 2, discussed above. Washing the feet of a guest in one's house was typically the duty of a servant. He who existed in equality with God became a servant among human beings and lowered Himself to wash the feet of those "enrolled in His school," His disciples. By doing this He both demonstrated His own submissiveness and provided an example for us to follow (verse 15). When you read this passage, hear once more the words of Jesus (freely rendered): "I am meek and lowly in heart; take on you the yoke of service I wear."

It may well be that Jesus chose this very time for the feet-washing because the disciples were on that same night arguing as to who of them would be greatest in the kingdom of God. Apparently right after that example He gave them this instruction: "The kings of the Gentiles exercise lordship over them.... But not so among you; on the contrary, he who is greatest among you, let him be as the younger, and he who governs as he who serves" (Luke 22:24-26). Jesus both acted in submissiveness and taught submissiveness for His disciples, including—perhaps *especially*—for the leaders.

Then, early on the dark night of His arrest and crucifixion, Jesus went into Gethsemane to pray. He was in heaviness of spirit, in such a strain that His perspiration was red with His blood. Understanding that His Father had prepared a "cup" for Him—the cup of human guilt, apparently, followed by God's judgment—He prayed three times, "Father, if it is Your will, take this cup from Me; nevertheless not My will, but Yours, be done" (Luke 22:42). Thus He submitted to do the Father's will: to drink the cup, to bear our sins to the cross, to experience the awful separation. All the submissiveness He showed so purely in the hours that followed grew out of this submissiveness to God in the Garden.

Emulating Jesus

Interestingly, Jesus demonstrated submissiveness in all the ways we should. He was subject to His parents as a child. He was subject to His God. He lowered Himself to wash the feet of His disciples. He showed submission toward others in bearing their sins in their place. He did not resist the governmental authorities who unjustly tried, sentenced, and executed Him.

There's a broad example in that for us, and the New Testament calls on us, as Jesus' disciples, to demonstrate the same submissiveness He demonstrated. Everything in this book grows out of that. And there's far more than I'm taking the space to discuss by name.

This doesn't mean that we never resist anything. Jesus did not yield His Father's house to be made a den of thieves without an active protest. We, too, will resist sin, anything that threatens God's place among us. But this book isn't about that.

This book, instead, is about the submissiveness our Lord expects us to emulate. So we ask ourselves this: In what ways should the example of Jesus in submissiveness inform us for our situations? How should submissiveness be exemplified in our lives, following in His steps (1 Peter 2:21)?

Some things are immediately clear. Like Jesus, we should not resist ill treatment suffered because of our commitment to Him. This is the lesson Peter drew in his first letter. Jesus Himself said that when we are persecuted for His sake we should not retaliate but should—in humility and meekness in practice—love and bless and do good to and pray for those who demonstrate their enmity to Christ in the way they treat us; see Matthew 5:10-12, 43-46. As we've seen above, this is the way Peter approaches the subject of being mistreated for Christ's sake; see also 1 Peter 4:13-14.

Equally clear is the fact that we—leaders first!—should love and serve others. This is so important that Jesus said others would know by this love that we are His disciples (John 13:35). And in biblical teaching, love is more than mere emotion; it is active and self-sacrificing, serving. Only those who are submissive—thinking of themselves as lowly and accepting their role in the expectations of others—will serve.

The rest of this book will call out other manifestations of submissiveness, and most of them will find practical meaning in applying the example of Jesus. For that matter, each reader can no doubt think of yet other ways this Christian grace should take effect.

Each one of us should ask ourselves a question like this one: If I am humble and meek and practice the grace of submissiveness, what will that look like in my life and in the actual situations I experience?

The words of Charles Wesley's hymn might have been originally intended for use by children. They work at least as well for all of us and touch on almost everything dealt with in this chapter. The hymn also makes a good prayer.

> Gentle Jesus, meek and mild,
> Look upon a little child;
> Pity my simplicity,
> Suffer me to come to Thee.
>
> Lamb of God, I look to Thee;
> Thou shalt my Example be;
> Thou art gentle, meek, and mild;
> Thou wast once a little child.
>
> Lord, I would be as Thou art;
> Give me Thine obedient heart;
> Thou art pitiful and kind,
> Let me have Thy loving mind.
>
> Let me, above all, fulfill
> God my heav'nly Father's will;
> Never His good Spirit grieve;
> Only to His glory live.

Loving Jesus, gentle Lamb,
In Thy gracious hands I am;
Make me, Savior, what Thou art,
Live Thyself within my heart.

("Gentle Jesus, Meek and Mild" by Charles Wesley)

Questions and suggestions for thought or discussion

- What does it mean to "wear the yoke" of Jesus?

- What are some things you learn from how Jesus Himself manifested submissiveness, and how you should put those lessons into practice in your own life?

- Which was the greater submission for Jesus, the incarnation or the crucifixion? Discuss the ways he showed submissiveness (humility or meekness) in both of these crucial events.

- Pick one of the three Synoptic Gospels—Matthew, Mark, or Luke—and read through the first ten chapters. Make a list of every instance when you think Jesus was demonstrating humility or meekness—whether the text actually says He was being humble (or meek) or not. Then consider how you might follow His example in the actual circumstances of your own life (whether at home, at work, at church, or otherwise), and write that down too.

Chapter 6

Submissiveness to God

So far, we have focused on general principles. Now we zero in on specific application of these principles, and doing this will provide the subject matter for several chapters.

Our first submissiveness is to God. All the rest builds on that because all the rest is commanded by Him and so demonstrates submission to Him.

The example of Jesus leaves no doubt that being submissive to God is paramount. He said His very sustenance was to do the will of the one who had sent Him (John 4:34; see also 5:30; 6:38, etc.). As we saw in the previous chapter, in Gethsemane on the night of His arrest He prayed three times, "Not my will, but thine be done." Jesus was in total submission to God, His Father.

James 4:7

The "golden text" for this chapter is from James 4:6-7: "God resists the proud, But gives grace to the humble. *Therefore sub-*

mit to God." That's what Peter meant when he said, "Fear God" (1 Peter 2:17). Indeed, Peter said almost the same thing James said: "God resists the proud, But gives grace to the humble. *Therefore humble yourselves under the mighty hand of God*" (1 Peter 5:5-6).

The verb *submit* means to put or place (or put in order) *under*, and so to subordinate oneself to another. It can therefore be accurately translated as submission or subjection. (Note that the English prefix *sub-* in all these words means *under*.)

The context for being in submission or subjection to God, in James, contributes to understanding the command. James is delivering a stern rebuke, denouncing those who have made themselves friends of the world (4:4). Instead, James admonishes, they ought to digest the words of Proverbs 3:34, "God resists the proud, but gives grace to the humble" (James 4:6). Consequently, they must submit to God and resist the devil.

The essential relationship between humility (*tapeinos*, lowliness) and submissiveness is thus made clear again; both are toward God. Resistance is the direct opposite of submission, just as pride is the direct opposite of humility. Some of James's readers, at least, have resisted God and submitted to the influences of the archenemy himself. Instead, they ought to resist that enemy and submit to God. If they humble themselves in this way, then God will not be in opposition to them—in their pride—but will give them grace to overcome their wicked ways.

Submission/Subjection in the New Testament

The verb translated *submit* or *be in subjection* (*hupotassō*) occurs more than 30 times in the Greek New Testament. It's a compound word, with the second part (*tassō*) meaning to *place* or *put* and the prefix (*hupo*) meaning *under*. The wide variety of usage, which I will only outline here—so that the reader can study it more thoroughly—helps us understand better the nature of submissiveness.[16]

More than a half dozen uses of the verb occur in reference to family relationships: wives to husbands (Ephesians 5:22; Colossians 3:18; Titus 2:5; 1 Peter 3:1, 5); children to parents (Luke 2:51, Jesus to His; in Ephesians and Colossians, when addressing children, Paul uses *honor* or *obey* instead of *submit/be subject to*); and bondservants to their masters (Titus 2:9; 1 Peter 2:18; Paul also uses *obey* instead of *submit* for this relationship). (Submission in family relationships will be the subject of a subsequent chapter in this volume.)

Sometimes the word appears in teaching about submission in church life (1 Corinthians 14:34; 16:16; Ephesians 5:21; 1 Peter 5:5). (Another chapter in this book will treat that subject.)

At other times the usage enjoins Christians to be in subjection to human government (Romans 13:1, 5; Titus 3:1; 1 Peter 2:13).

---

[16] The cognate noun for subjection or submission (*hupotagē*) occurs only four or five times and adds nothing to the study of the verb presented here. It appears in 2 Corinthians 9:13 ("obedience"), Galatians 2:5, 1 Timothy 2:11; 3:4. The last two, like several uses of the verb described in this study, refer to the submission of wives to husbands and of children to parents, respectively.

(This work will also devote a chapter to the matter of submission in respect to governing authorities.)

One fairly large number of uses of the word reflects Psalm 8:6, which promises, in reference to humanity and the created order: "You [God] have put all things under his [man's] feet" (cf. Genesis 1:28); God has subjected all creation to mankind. The New Testament applies this in a special way to that greatest of human beings, the Son of Man, interpreting it to mean that all things have and will be brought into subjection to Jesus Christ (1 Corinthians 15:27-28; Ephesians 1:22; Hebrews 2:5, 8; and possibly Philippians 3:21 and 1 Peter 3:22). Although this highly interesting group of passages goes beyond the primary interest of the present chapter, it still serves to fill out our understanding of the basic meaning of submissiveness.

Most of the rest of the uses of this verb fit no specific categories. Jesus' disciples rejoiced that demons were *subject to* the name of Christ (Luke 10:17), but Jesus cautioned them against pride in the fact that the spirits were *subject to* them (Luke 10:20). Paul affirmed that the unsaved, as those who live in accord with the flesh, are not and cannot be *in subjection to* the law of God (Romans 8:7). Subsequently in the same chapter Paul observes that the created order is *in subjection to* "futility" (verse 20)—apparently meaning that the cosmos itself suffers as a result of the curse. Paul also reveals that Israel's rejection by God is not arbitrary but for good reason: namely, because they have not *submitted* to the righteousness God has provided by faith in Christ (Romans 10:3; cf. 9:32). In an entirely different context, Paul indicates that the spirits of prophets are *subject to* the prophets themselves: that is, to their own self-control and will (1 Corinthians 14:32). As broad as this group is, the passages point to a clear meaning for subjection or submission: namely, as obedience to that which prevails or is in control or has authority.

Finally, two other uses of the word are essentially equivalent to submission to God. (1) Just as we have been in subjection to our earthly parents, so we ought to submit to the one who is our Father spiritually (Hebrews 12:9). (2) The church is in subjection to Christ, the Second Person of the Godhead (Ephesians 5:24).

Submissiveness Toward God as Obedience

Once we grant the biblical teaching that we are to be in submission to God, the need to define what this means arises. Perhaps the single, most basic thing it means is that we are to *obey* God. Indeed, the Greek lexicon that defines the verb (*hupotassō*) to mean *submit* or *be subject to,* also gives *obey* as a good translation of the word itself. If you look over the list of uses of this verb, given in the preceding section, you will have no difficulty substituting *obey* in many of them.

Humility and meekness, as discussed in chapters 1 and 2, are directly involved in obedience, of course. One who thinks highly of himself (Romans 12:3), the opposite of humility, will not quickly obey anyone else, including God. The very essence of pride is to insist on having one's way. However, if we see ourselves as lowly and then respond to God meekly, we will submit to Him. That will entail, by definition, *obedience.*

The word for *submissiveness* doesn't have to be present in a passage for us to see an example of submissiveness toward God. Consider the human parents of Jesus. Mary, whose experience I will return to in a subsequent chapter on biblical examples, responded to the incredible words of the angel Gabriel: "Behold the maidservant of the Lord! Let it be to me according to your word" (Luke 1:38). In other words, she did exactly what James 4:7 asks; she bowed in obedient submission to God.

Mary's husband-to-be, Joseph, was no less an obedient, submissive Christian. His story is in Matthew 1:18-25. Knowing nothing of Gabriel's visit to Mary he learns of Mary's pregnancy and sees it for what it has to mean as far as he and others can tell—she has been with another man. There is nothing to do but divorce her, although out of a generous spirit that already reveals his humility he will do that as quietly as possible. But an angel comes and explains what has really happened and points out the Scripture that is being fulfilled. Ah! That makes all the difference, and Joseph "did as the angel of the Lord commanded him and took to him his wife" (verse 24) in wholehearted, submissive obedience. Furthermore, in his humility and meekness, he denied himself the pleasure of becoming "one flesh" with her for many months to come (verse 25).

That wasn't the end of obedience for either of them. Joseph showed himself especially sensitive and submissive to whatever the Lord asked; see Matthew 1:21, 23; 2:13-14; 2:19-21 for other proofs.

Submitting to God in obedience means we intend to observe all things He has commanded (Matthew 28:19-20). This isn't exactly the same thing as keeping all the details of the Mosaic Law, whose structure no longer governs the life of those justified by faith in Jesus Christ. It is our duty to discern all the moral judgments of God for our conduct wherever they are found in His word—in the Mosaic Law and elsewhere. And obeying Him, as He expressed His will—His law—in these moral judgments is perhaps the most important way we express, by faith, our submissiveness to God. I am not referring to sinless perfection, but I am saying that without characteristic obedience we cannot claim to be submissive to God—and therefore cannot with justification claim to be Christians.[17]

Sometimes obedience is dangerous, even threatening death. When in the early days of the church Peter and John were commanded by their Jewish authorities to cease proclaiming Jesus, they said, "Whether it is right in the sight of God to listen to you more than to God, you judge. For we cannot but speak the things which we have seen and heard" (Acts 4:19-20). When Shadrach, Meshach, and Abed-Nego were commanded to bow down to Nebuchadnezzar's image, they answered, "Our God whom we serve is able to deliver us from the burning fiery furnace, and He will deliver us.... But if not, let it be known to you, O king, that we do not serve your gods" (Daniel 3:17-18). Obeying God could have cost any of these their lives, but they did so anyway.

Sometimes submitting to God in obedience involves great uncertainty about the outcome. Hebrews 11:8 reports that Abraham, by faith, when called to go away from his homeland to a place God would show him, "obeyed" and "went out, not knowing where he was going." His submissiveness was expressed as obedience, and this in turn expressed his faith.

---

[17] For a volume establishing this understanding see my *Discipleship: The Expression of Saving Faith* (Nashville: Randall House, 2013).

Obeying God isn't limited to His commandments recorded in the Bible, although that's where it starts. This kind of submission is called for when we find ourselves confident that God is asking something of us or directing us in a certain way or calling us to some service. Such leadings as these are not quite as easy to be sure about as the commandments in Scripture; impressions are often subjective and we can be wrong in what we think we sense. Nevertheless, there are "leadings" that we recognize as from God, and when that is the case our submissiveness again takes the form of obedience.

Submissiveness Toward God as Accepting His Providential Arrangement of Our Circumstances

The providence of God means that He is managing *all* the circumstances of our lives. Romans 8:28 assures us that He is doing this *for good*: that is, for the achievement of His purpose for us: namely, to bring us into conformity with the image of His Son, to re-shape us in character and personality. Although we are often unable to determine just how He is working and how the circumstances He places us in will be for our ultimate good, our confidence in Him and His all-encompassing control of things means that we will submit to where He has placed us and the circumstances we are in.

Defining just how this works isn't always easy. Submitting to His providential arrangement of the circumstances of our lives doesn't mean, for example, that when we are sick we simply accept the fact and avoid the doctor or the medicine the doctor prescribes. The circumstances we find ourselves in are often challenges to work for something better. But when we have done our best in ways we believe He would have us be active to change our circumstances, we leave the results to Him and accept what turns out to be His will in the matter.

If we find that our sickness can't be cured, for example, we don't rebel against God. Instead, we submit to the hand of Providence in our circumstances. If He places us in a difficult situation or location, one we can't change, or we can't gain peace that He would have us change it, we submit to what He has arranged for us and remain faithful.

This, too, is a form of obedience, and such obedience is often hard.

Perhaps the best biblical illustration of such submission to God is found in the example of Jesus Himself. He knew very well that He was going to be crucified in Jerusalem; Matthew 20:17-19 records just one of many instances when He made this known, in advance, to His disciples. But when His "hour" had come, as He expressed it, He was weighed down with what He faced, understanding what was held in "the cup" He was about to drink. No doubt He recognized that the sins of the world would be put on Him and He would experience the soul-wrenching pain of separation from His Father, the holy God who cannot look with favor on sin. Understandably, He shrank from that experience and prayed, "O My Father, if it is possible, let this cup pass from Me; nevertheless, not as I will, but as You will" (Matthew 26:39). The agony was so great that His sweat was like drops of blood, the Bible says.

Such was His submission. And such should be ours. One does not hear the voice of God in submission and then disobey; by definition, to do so is a contradiction.

Another Biblical Example of Submission to God

I have already mentioned, using Hebrews 11:8, the obedience of Abraham when God called him from Ur to go to a place he did not know. The same chapter relates an even more astounding example of his submissive obedience (11:17-18), summarizing the story originally narrated in Genesis 22:1-19.

The unthinkable thing has transpired: God Himself is testing Abraham (Hebrews confirms) and directs him to sacrifice Isaac. To appreciate this fully, one must remember the background. For years and years, God had promised Abraham a son through whom a huge lineage would be his heirs, a people through whom all the nations would be blessed. Not until Abraham and Sarah were both past child-bearing age did God fulfill this promise, bringing Isaac into this world as the precious, promised seed. The record shows clearly that Isaac was the laughter of Sarah and the light of Abraham's eye.

And God has asked what it would seem He cannot ask. Abraham must take the young man—perhaps in his late teens now—to a place where God will show him, and offer Isaac there as a sacrifice to God. This is against the very law of God, against the role this unique son has been promised in the plan of God; yet there is no doubt that the voice requiring this is God Himself.

Does Abraham object? We would not be surprised, but the record does not indicate so. Does he weep and pray? Perhaps, but again the record is silent. As far as we can tell, he obeys with alacrity. Regardless, he obeys. He and Isaac and two servants set out early one morning and on the third day, they stop in sight of the place, Mount Moriah. With heavy heart, no doubt, he leaves the servants there and proceeds to the place where he will do God's awful bidding.

To be sure, he does this in faith. The submissive obedience itself is the expression of his faith. And he has a certain confidence that God will restore Isaac to him after the bloody deed is done. He tells the servants, "We will come back to you." Hebrews 11:19 says he believed God was able to raise Isaac from the dead. This verb (*logizomai*) means to reckon, calculate, consider. Abraham figured, he counted on, God to restore Isaac to life after he sacrificed him. That, too, was part of his faith.

There is no question whether Abraham actually intended to make Isaac a burnt offering. Even in counting on God's power to restore life he was planning for Isaac's death. He built the required altar, laid the wood for the fire on it, and bound Isaac, then placed him on the altar. He raised the knife he had brought for the purpose, perhaps one he, as priest for his family, reserved for the sacred service of sacrifice. And if God had not stopped him the young man would have bled to death from the severing of his jugular and would have been burned there. Hebrews says that Abraham, when he was tested, "offered up Isaac ... his only begotten son." In his heart the obedience was complete.

This is a challenging example of submission to God! We are assured that we will not be called on in exactly the same way—but we will be called on. We already have been. We must offer ourselves to God as *living* sacrifices, refusing to let the world press us into its mold, getting our thought-processes renewed at every step to discern and test out God's will in our lives every day (Romans 12:1-2). That is what we should learn from the example of Abraham.

Concluding Overview:
The Nature of Our Submission to God

What are the dimensions of our submission to God? Here is a concluding, summary overview of the major elements of that submission. Some have already been touched on, and you may be able to think of yet other elements.

1. *Submission to God is trusting His provision for our salvation without offering Him our works.* Saving faith is one manifestation of submission to God. By nature we are proud and prefer to do for ourselves. Pride gets in the way of humbly acknowledging that we are not able to save ourselves, that we are sinners. Self-assertion keeps us from accepting that there is nothing we can do that will deliver us from the power and penalty of our sins. Our self-confidence holds us back from meekly accepting that God has already done the work, that He has provided in grace His Son as atonement for our sins.

For an excellent example of this see what Paul said, in Romans 9-11, when he discussed the failure of many Jews, in his day, to achieve right standing with God. They have failed, he said, to attain righteousness before God (9:31). Why? Because they sought to do so by their own *works* (9:32). They were "seeking to establish their own righteousness" and had "not *submitted* to the righteousness" that God Himself has provided (10:3).

Don't forget what Jesus said: "Unless you are converted and become as little children, you will by no means enter the kingdom of heaven. Therefore whoever *humbles himself* as this little child is the greatest in the kingdom of heaven" (Matthew 18:3-4). James 4:6 says God "gives grace—which includes *saving* grace—to the *humble*." 1 Peter 5:6 urges, "*Humble* yourselves under the mighty hand of God, that He may exalt you in due time." That exalting ultimately lifts us to Heaven.

2. *Submission to God is ordering our lives by His law without rebellion against His authority.* Doing this, as I've claimed earlier in this chapter, is a matter of *obedience.* I want to emphasize, now, that we *are* "under the law of God."

Sure, there's a sense in which we are *not* under the Law. We are not under the governance of the *Mosaic Law* as a system that orders our lives. The Mosaic Law was ordained for the nation of Israel in the Old Testament period, and it included civil and ceremonial laws as well as moral laws. As a life-ordering system, it was but a "schoolmaster" (or tutor or guardian) to bring us to Christ, and we are no longer under that system (Galatians 3:24-25).

Even so, we are under God's law. As citizens of the Kingdom of God, we are in the domain over which He rules and subject to His authority. He has the right to govern our lives, and submitting to Jesus as our Savior by definition means submitting to Him as our Lord. That means we're subject to all His moral judgments. Some are identical with items in the Mosaic Law, but all are in the teachings of Jesus, whose disciples we are. He is the one who said that becoming disciples entails observing all the things He commanded (Matthew 28:19-20). Jesus is Lord.

Saying this does not mean we are saved by works. We do not obey Him to earn His favor, in hopes that our obedience will be rewarded with Heaven. That would take us back to self-asserting pride that we can save ourselves. No, living in obedience to God is an expression of our saving faith; it's obeying because we trust and love and serve—*submit* to—Him.

For a good expression of this kind of life, take note how Luke described Zacharias and Elizabeth, the parents of John the Baptist: "They were both righteous before God, walking in all the commandments and ordinances of the Lord blameless" (Luke 1:6). No wonder they submitted to God in naming and rearing their special son!

3. *Submission to God is being satisfied with what He provides for us without discontent and grumbling.* This truth isn't one-sided, of course. The very governance of the Lord that we submit to includes His design that we work to earn our way, to feed and clothe and shelter ourselves. From the beginning God ordained work, even before the fall of Adam and Eve. Paul said, "If anyone will not work, neither shall he eat" (2 Thessalonians 3:10).

Even so, the Bible teaches that it is ultimately God who provides for us, and with His provision we should be satisfied. There's an intriguing statement about this in Hebrews 13:5: "Let your conduct be without covetousness; be content with such things as you have. For He Himself has said, 'I will never leave you nor forsake you.'"

One of the clear implications of this verse is that dissatisfaction with what one has is the root of discontent, and that, in turn, leads to covetousness. Another clear implication is that such dissatisfaction is, at root, dissatisfaction with God Himself. It is He who accepts responsibility for our well-being. Consequently to complain or to fear is to distrust God.

4. *Submission to God is accepting the circumstances He arranges for us without bitterness or distrust.* This is the same as the preceding, only broader. It takes us back to the section, earlier in the chapter, where we dealt with accepting God's providential arrangement of our circumstances. I bring it up again now for another word.

God's providence is at work in everything that involves us. As I've said already, Romans 8:28 promises us that He is at work in *all* things for our good.

Among other things, this means that we must accept everything that comes our way as being by His hand. That doesn't excuse us from our own responsibility, of course. If we are neglectful, or make a careless mistake, or do wrong, there will be consequences that we have brought on ourselves. Nevertheless, even in such circumstances God is at work.

Our problem, then, is that sometimes we don't like our circumstances. Things don't go the way we wanted them to. A loved one dies. We are diagnosed with cancer or something worse. We lose a job, whether from our own failing or through no fault of our own. Is God at work in such circumstances? Yes, God's providence includes everything, even when we can't make any sense of things.

This doesn't mean that we don't work to improve our circumstances; we do. But sometimes nothing we do helps. The danger is that we will blame God or turn away from Him altogether. Submissiveness to God means we resist that temptation and accept what He brings our way without bitterness or distrust of Him.

Paul set a good example in this in the way he handled what he called his "thorn in the flesh" (see 2 Corinthians 12:7-10). We don't know what that was, apparently some physical malady. Three times he asked God to take it away, but that prayer went unanswered. Instead, God helped him to understand that the "thorn" was for his good, to keep him from pride and to cause him to learn to depend on God's help. In the end, submitting to God, he was able to affirm the sufficiency of grace and that the power of Jesus was made manifest in his own personal weakness. He learned to rejoice in trials and in the glorification of his Lord.

5. *Submission to God is serving God, and doing so without "kicking over the traces."* This takes us back, finally, to the invitation of Jesus, "Take my yoke upon you, and learn of me, for I am meek and lowly in heart." A yoke is a harness for a work animal, like an ox. A yoke makes it possible to use and control the animal for service of one sort or another, whether pulling a wagon or a plow.

So what does it mean to "serve the Lord"? It's a perfectly good and common biblical expression, appearing there often and in both testaments. The idea is at the heart of Joshua's closing challenge to Israel: "Choose for yourselves this day whom you will *serve* ... But as for me and my house, we will *serve* the Lord" (Joshua 24:15). The people answered: "We also will *serve* the Lord, for He is our God" (verse 18). This was in deliberate contrast, both on

Joshua's part and the people's part, with *serving* other gods (verses 14, 16).

Many other instances could be cited. Psalm 100:2 invites us, "*Serve* the Lord with gladness; Come before His presence with singing." The "three Hebrew children," resisting Nebuchadnezzar's intimidation, said, "Our God whom we *serve* is able to deliver us" (Daniel 3:17). In Matthew 6:24 Jesus said, "You cannot *serve* God and mammon." In a ship doomed to be wrecked, Paul spoke to the crew and passengers about "the God to whom I belong and whom I *serve* (Acts 27:23). Paul wrote the Thessalonians, remembering that they had "turned to God from idols, to *serve* the living and true God" (1 Thessalonians 1:9).

Serving the Lord stands in direct contrast to serving any other god. It often refers to one's worship, allegiance, obedient conduct, or ministry. In short, serving the Lord means ordering one's life under the authority and will of the Trinitarian God and in submission to Him. Serving the Lord is living for Him and doing His bidding out of love and loyalty to Him; it includes everything discussed in this chapter.

I grew up on a farm and we worked mules. Instead of a yoke we had a bridle that included bits in the mule's mouth that the reins were tied to. On the shoulders of the mule was a large, leather collar, and anchored to it, on each side, were "traces": long chains that could be hooked to whatever the mule was pulling. Sometimes a mule would get agitated or ornery and step out of the traces on one side or the other. That created a serious mess, leaving the mule straddling the trace on one side or the other, unable to pull. That was called "kicking over (or out of) the traces," an expression that has come to stand for rebellion and refusal to submit. May the Spirit of God keep us humble and meek, submitting to the yoke of Jesus and faithfully obeying and serving "in the traces."

Questions and suggestions for thought or discussion

- Are humility and meekness necessarily involved in obeying God? Why?

- Name some ways our submission to God will involve obedience to Him.

- Give examples when you did or did not obey God, both in what He has said in the Bible and in some individual leading you experienced, and what resulted from that.

- Describe a time when you found yourself in circumstances that were so difficult that you wanted to rebel against them. Did you submit to God as being in control? Perhaps on some such occasion, the difficult thing turned out for good; if so, talk about that.

- Make a list, written or mental, of the last two times you believe you disobeyed God. If you haven't confessed them as sins, do so now and commit to God not to disobey Him in those circumstances (or different ones) again.

- Make a list of two times you believe you submitted/obeyed when God was prompting you in your spirit to do one thing or another. Evaluate how it turned out.

- In practical terms, what does it mean to "serve" the Lord?

- Write down a half dozen things you believe are involved in "serving" the Lord. Evaluate how you're doing in these matters.

Chapter 7

Submissiveness to Governmental Authorities

here are several passages in the New Testament that command Christians to demonstrate submission toward those who govern. These include two relatively short instructions in Titus 3:1 and 1 Peter 2:13-17 and a more detailed one in Romans 13:1-7. All three use the very word for submission or being in subjection (*hupotassō*) that serves to give focus to this work and which we examined in the previous chapter.

I include here the text of the passages in Titus and 1 Peter, with the English words that translate this Greek word underlined. These verses say almost nothing that is not contained in Romans 13, so my main approach in this chapter will be to expound that most helpful and detailed passage in Romans.

Titus 3:1:

Remind them to <u>be subject to</u> rulers and authorities, to
obey, to be ready for every good work.

1 Peter 2:13-17:

[13] Therefore <u>submit</u> yourselves to every ordinance of man
for the Lord's sake, whether to the king as supreme, [14]
or to governors, as to those who are sent by him for the
punishment of evildoers and *for the* praise of those who
do good. [15] For this is the will of God, that by doing good
you may put to silence the ignorance of foolish men—[16]
as free, yet not using liberty as a cloak for vice, but as
bondservants of God. [17] Honor all *people*. Love the brotherhood. Fear God. Honor the king.

Romans 13:1-7

Again, the same word for submission or subjection is key, and
it occurs twice: first in verse 1 as the injunction is introduced, and
again in verse 5 as the concluding summary is emphasized.

[1] Let every soul <u>be subject to</u> the governing authorities.
For there is no authority except from God, and the authorities that exist are appointed by God. [2] Therefore
whoever resists the authority resists the ordinance of
God, and those who resist will bring judgment on themselves. [3] For rulers are not a terror to good works, but to
evil. Do you want to be unafraid of the authority? Do
what is good, and you will have praise from the same. [4]
For he is God's minister to you for good. But if you do
evil, be afraid; for he does not bear the sword in vain;

for he is God's minister, an avenger to *execute* wrath on him who practices evil. [5] Therefore *you* must <u>be subject</u>, not only because of wrath but also for conscience' sake. [6] For because of this you also pay taxes, for they are God's ministers attending continually to this very thing. [7] Render therefore to all their due: taxes to whom taxes *are due,* customs to whom customs, fear to whom fear, honor to whom honor.

My purpose is primarily to expound this passage in order to draw out its lessons for us as citizens of the kingdom of God ordered to be in submission to a kingdom that is of this world. We can define this in two main parts.

The Place of Governing Authorities

In defining this, Paul makes three main observations.

1. *Governing authorities have been put in place by God.* This is said twice for emphasis. Verse 1 says they are "appointed by God" (NKJV) or "ordained of God" (KJV), which means the same thing. Literally, the word (*tassomai*) means they have been put in place. God has positioned them where they are. Verse 2 says any resistance to them is resistance to the "ordinance of God," which is another word on the same root.

God Almighty has arranged for there to be worldly authorities—governmental structures and persons to administer them. That's part of the order of society that He has determined is best for human beings, enabling them to live together without chaos.

We must not underestimate the importance of this divine arrangement.

2. *Governing authorities are ministers of God.* This is said three times to make sure we get the point. In verse 4 the one governing is twice referred to as God's minister (*diakonos*). Verse 6 repeats it again in English, but it is a different Greek word (*leitourgoi*). Both words involve *service* or *ministry*, but the one in verse 6 is more formal and often refers to religious or priestly service.

We need to recognize that presidents and governors and congressmen and judges and policemen are *in the ministry*! Verse 6 says the authorities are "attending continually to this very thing": that is, to this ministry. They are *in full-time ministry*!

Yes, I know that this means they are in God's *service*, but that's all the word *ministry* means even when we're describing ordained ministers who preach the gospel. Those who govern, too, are ministers, ordained not by the church but by God Himself. They exercise responsibility and authority in civil government and minister for (or serve) God in doing so.

3. *Governing authorities are in place to punish and reward.* There are four phrases here; interesting that three are about punishment and only one about reward. Perhaps that's because evil is the human tendency. The great Christian thinker Augustine said that government is a necessary evil, necessary because of evil.

Verse 3: "a terror not to good works, but to evil (works)." Those who govern are there to strike fear in the hearts of those who are tempted to do wrong.

Verse 4: "an avenger to execute wrath on him who practices evil." Romans 12:19 says, "Vengeance is mine, I will repay, says the Lord." In civil matters, however, the governing authorities do this work for God; that's one of the ways they are His ministers. They are agents to express God's wrath on those who do wrong.

Verse 4: "does not bear the sword in vain." It doesn't hang from the officer's side just for show! He has the right and the power to exact punishment on law-breakers, including the power to execute them.

Verse 3 again [my translation]: "Do you desire not to be terrified by the authority? Then be practicing what is good and you will have praise from the authority." If we want the approval of those who govern us, if we want to avoid the fines and the prisons and the gas chamber, and anything else that's part of "the long arm of the law," then all we have to do is what's right. Obey the law. That's the main part of the required submission.

1 Peter 2:14 said, in effect: "Submit to governors, as to those who have been sent by God for the punishment or avenging of evildoers and praise of good-doers." Those are the same words as here; I suspect that Peter was quoting Paul.

This is the major work of civil authorities: to keep down wrongdoing and promote the practice of doing right. Sometimes I wish all those in government realized this, since they get involved in so much more—although my purpose now does not include critiquing the way our government functions. But if they accomplish this basic thing, keeping down wrong and promoting right, they're serving God in doing so—if they punish and so deter crime, injustice, stealing, cheating, murder, lying, adultery, and all other sorts of wickedness; and if they thereby promote honesty, respect for life, fidelity, and justice, and all other sorts of upright behavior.

Of course, they do this with some degree of success, and they fail in some measure. But God has placed them in power for that reason, and working to accomplish that purpose is their ministry—even if they don't acknowledge God, although they should. We affirm them in that divinely ordained role. As Christians, we recognize that the rule of God lies behind the rule of men and it is our duty to live in a way that matches that recognition.

The Place of Christians in Respect to Civil Authorities

This is the second major element of Romans 13:1-7. There are four things we can draw from what Paul says.

1. The first of these is the most basic, undergirding all the rest: *we are to be in a position of submission* to civil authority. To keep us from missing this, Paul says it twice—in verse 1 and again in verse 5, as already noted—and it's his very first word on the subject. Literally, the word (*hypotassomai*) means "to place or position oneself under"; that is, under the governing authorities. It's the exact opposite of the word *resist* in verse 2, which is to place or position oneself against.

Paul gives us two reasons for this in verse 5: first, "because of the wrath." That is, the wrath that the authority exercises on behalf of God in punishing wrongdoing. We are to be in submission to the authorities lest that wrath fall on us.

The other reason is "for conscience' sake." That is because the authorities represent God and we don't want to be in resistance to the ordinance of God. We will violate our conscience before God

Himself if we rebel against the governmental authorities He has put in place.

The first reason is a practical one, the second is an abiding principle. For both reasons, our God requires that we live in submission to the laws of the land and those who administer them.

2. The second thing about our place is this: *We are to do what is good.* Verse 3: if you want to be able to live without fear of the officers of the law, do what's good. And then you'll receive praise, not punishment. Verse 4 says he is a minister of God to us "for good." Probably that means to get us to do what is good, but it's also for our own good!

That's the same thing Paul says in Titus 3:1: "Remind them to be subject to rulers and authorities, to obey, to be ready for every good work."

Our submission, then, takes the form of obedience to the law, and this should result in a heart that is eager to do what is right in the sight of God and man as upheld by our laws.

3. The third thing about our place in relation to governing authorities is that *we are to pay for their services.* This may be unpopular, but it's here in God's Word: "Render therefore to all their due: taxes to whom taxes are due, customs to whom customs."

Jesus said to give to Caesar the things that are Caesar's (Matthew 22:21). Important: in context, that came when He was asked about paying taxes! Why? Well, remember that those in government are in the *full-time* ministry of God, and it's our duty to support their ministry!

Sure, we often wonder about how they spend our taxes, and where we have legitimate opportunities we can try to get such things changed. But in the end, we should pay our taxes cheerfully, recognizing that by doing so we are supporting the order that God Himself has established. This, too, is the form our submission takes.

4. The fourth and final thing about our place is this: *We are to respect the civil authorities.* Verse 7 continues: "fear to whom fear [is due], honor to whom honor [is due]." 1 Peter 2:17 said, "Honor the king."

By now the basis for this is clear. Those in civil authority are ministers of God, acting as His servants to uphold law and order, deter evil, and foster uprightness. They may not be perfect, they may not even know God personally, but they are functioning as an essential mechanism in His providential government of the created order. We ought, therefore, to show them the respect they deserve for the responsible role they have. Even when we can't respect a given individual, we can respect the office he or she holds.

Again, this is what it means for us to demonstrate submissiveness.

Application

At this point, I feel constrained to make an observation that is important for us Christians to be fully aware of. The officers of the law—whether presidents or governors or congressmen or judges, and including police officers—are sinners like all the rest of us, depraved human beings. Many of them are not living in submission to God personally. No matter how well trained, how disciplined, they are as imperfect and fallible and subject to human emotions and temptations as any other human beings. Realizing this, and taking Romans 13 into account, means at least two things.

On the one hand, it means that we will not be surprised when a police officer, for example, gun in hand, loses his temper and abuses or even kills someone without full justification. Or when a president or other elected official is exposed for corruption or sexual sin.

On the other hand, Romans 13 means that we will not be quick to judge, that we will give them respect for the office they occupy, at least until they have certainly forfeited it.

And I think it means that we will be temperate in our criticism of civil authorities, being careful not to engender disrespect and ridicule. I cringe sometimes when I hear fellow Christians talking about some government official, like our president, or referring to "government" as though that's some bad thing.

Remember what Paul says: civil authorities stand in the place of God over us. They are there as part of His providential government of our social order. Both as citizens and as Christians we owe them our obedience and support and respect.

I must acknowledge, again, that I have only set out the *principles* that are here, not so much how to apply them. Frankly, I don't feel all that guilty about this, primarily because I believe that if we get the principles right, if we fix them firmly in our minds and make a serious effort to work out the details, we will manage the application acceptably. We may not all apply them in exactly the same ways, but if we are conscientious about the principles we won't be that far apart in application.

Now, in conclusion, let me offer a few practical observations that go beyond Paul and Peter. I trust they are grounded in biblical principles.

1. The Bible does not define the form of government that is ideal. Israel, of course, was meant to be governed as a theocracy, with God as their King. Even when they inaugurated the monarchy with human kings, those kings were still supposed to be subject to the direct governance of God.

There are some Christian thinkers, today, who propose that we ought to institute "theonomy," as they call it, meaning government by God as He has revealed Himself in the Christian Bible. The word *theonomy* simply means the law of God. Muslims, in a similar way, believe we should be governed by God as defined in the Qu'ran, that the earthly state should institute *sharia* law. Either of these, theonomy or sharia, would cancel the separation of powers that I'll refer to in the following.

But the Bible, while it taught theocracy for Israel, doesn't speak to the issue of what form of government is best. It doesn't demand monarchy, oligarchy (government by a small, elite number), a republic, or even a democracy. When Paul wrote Romans, he wasn't speaking of a democratic form of government—or any other certain form. We must not think that "civil religion" will take us to Heaven. God can and does work in the lives of people who live in a dictatorship as well as among those in a democracy. Whatever the form of government, the principles of our submission and support apply. It is not the purpose of Christian faith to demand democracy—or any other form of government.

2. There are limits, of course, to our obedience of civil government. But the only limit that is clearly approved by the Word of God is this: when a civil government requires us to disobey God, we obey God rather than men. That's exactly what Peter and John said when the Jewish Sanhedrin attempted to silence them from proclaiming the gospel (Acts 5:29), and Jesus Christ Himself had commanded them to spread the good news of His redemptive work.

In speaking about this qualification, we must remember that it's easy for us, sometimes, to confuse our preferences with what God requires. He hasn't necessarily called our churches to be tax-exempt, for example. Regardless, we can be grateful we live under a government that isn't likely to require us to disobey God, at least not for now.

3. I suggest that we should also be grateful that we live in a land where there is a separation of powers between the church and the state. Theologian R. C. Sproul explains this means that both are answerable to God, but they have separate jobs. The church doesn't enforce laws against crimes in society and administer punishment for them, maintain armies to defend our freedom, or define the rules of the road. The state doesn't do evangelism, baptize converts, pay pastors, or discipline heretics.

But if the state, like the church, is answerable to God for how it does its job, then that means that in the end even government is not really free to operate independently of Him. Let's say that one of the functions of government is to ensure that justice rules in human affairs. Even defining what justice is depends on God's revelation of Himself in the created order and human conscience. That's what we call *natural law*.

Furthermore, if there's a separation of powers, the implication is that there is a separation of our personal roles. Some things we ought to do as Christians, and some as citizens of our country. And while we can't separate these entirely, or take either one of them out from under our submission to God, there is a basic difference between the two realms, between Caesar's kingdom and God's.

4. The New Testament doesn't speak to us about how we *participate* in our government. This means, I think, that how we participate is something we do as citizens rather than as Christians—although, of course, our Christian character will govern how we conduct ourselves in every way, including how we participate as citizens of our country.

Paul and Peter wrote to people who had no opportunity to participate in their government. They couldn't run for office. They couldn't vote for those who would govern them. They couldn't sponsor referendums about laws and enforcement. They couldn't sit on juries and decide guilt or innocence or punishment. They couldn't circulate petitions to get this or that changed. They couldn't march in protests when officials overextended themselves.

We can do all of these things. Should we? How can we determine how to vote as Christians, say, when no candidate takes a trustworthy stand for godliness?

There have been those in the history of the Christian church who have said we should not participate at all. Some would say,

"We have to withdraw from all involvement with any Political System, by turning in our voter's registration cards, and having our names expunged from the voting rolls; by doing this we are then REPENTING of the evil, and making a stand for God."

But other Christians, past and present, have said that it is our duty *as citizens* to participate, to vote, to seek in whatever ways our government provides for us, as citizens, to influence our government for right. If, as I've said, it is a major function of government to promote justice, then, in all the broad implications of that word *justice*, as Christian citizens, recognizing justice as a fundamental quality God Himself has ordained, we ought to work for the fullest implementations of justice possible.

How then shall we vote? I don't know. At least I don't know insofar as voting for specific persons or parties is concerned. It is more than theoretically possible, sometimes, that one candidate who is not a Christian may govern better than another who is. Which matters most, we ask ourselves, a person's character or his or her philosophy of government? Both matter, and perhaps equally! And that leaves us with tough decisions for which there are no simple guidelines. Is the party "platform" important? Certainly, but perhaps that consideration doesn't outweigh all others. Participating in government, by definition, is momentous, and momentous things aren't always easy or obvious, even for Christians.

Even as Christians, living in the USA and functioning within the two-party system that prevails at the moment (which isn't to say that it necessarily should, only that it does), we don't confuse the earthly kingdom with the kingdom of God. To be sure, *one day all the kingdoms of this world will become the kingdom of our God and of His Christ! AMEN!* (See Revelation 11:15.) Meanwhile, if we want to know how to vote, then we vote in the way we think will best promote God's revealed will, including justice, in the earthly order we're privileged to participate in.

Can we participate beyond voting? Certainly, but merely being a Christian doesn't serve as a basis for decisions along these lines. We can always write letters to editors, for example, and they don't necessarily have to be about "Christian" issues. We can volunteer to work for a candidate we support. We can even work for a candidate or party professionally, or run for office ourselves. There are many ways to make our voices heard in the public square, and as Americans we live in a country where there are many such opportunities.

I remember when my pastor was going to be out of town at the time an establishment just up the hill from us was being heard on its application for a license to sell beer. Pastor asked me to go to the meeting and represent our church, which was nearer than any other to that establishment. I did, and I was almost floored when the chairman of the "beer board" (as it was popularly called) started the meeting with *prayer*! I had to give that some thought, but I finally realized that a Christian could, indeed, preside over the granting of licenses to sell alcoholic beverages. If the law of the land provides for such licenses, then some government entity has to oversee that provision and should do so with integrity and an even hand, regardless of how the people in that office feel about drinking. A beer board could, at least in theory, be made up of all Christians, even teetotalers, and yet administer such a provision;

as I'm about to emphasize, the board, as such, isn't a Christian, after all.

5. It is important to keep in mind that government, at any level—any governing entity, that is—*is not a Christian and does not function in accord with the principles by which persons, as Christians, function.* The very best proof of this lies in what the Bible teaches about *vengeance.* "Vengeance is mine, I will repay, says the Lord," which the inspired Paul applies to mean that we are not to avenge ourselves (Romans 12:19). And yet, a few verses later the same inspired Paul says that a governing official is in place to serve as "an avenger to execute wrath" on the one who does wrong (Romans 13:4).

As individual Christians, we are to forgive those who sin. Government exists to punish them and so to deter wrongdoing. Christians are to manifest "the fruit of the Spirit," as in Galatians 5:22-23, and so they will love their enemies and show compassion in ways the government cannot and should not. It is a confusion of two distinct realms to try to evaluate every government policy (or even government officials) by the standards of Christian conduct and character. When facing issues that involve human needs and rights, government acts in accord with its constitutional mandate to seek the public good and general welfare, to protect rights, to ensure justice, to provide safety. Sometimes those interests can be tailored in accord with the things Jesus commanded His disciples; sometimes they can't. In our public debates about policies and laws, it's freeing to realize that the objectives of government are not necessarily the objectives of the church.

6. And finally, there is yet one thing the Bible makes clear. Our inspired writer Paul, in 1 Timothy 2:1-2, says, "I exhort first of all that supplications, prayers, intercessions, *and* giving of thanks be made for all men, for kings and all who are in authority, that we may lead a quiet and peaceable life in all godliness and reverence." We are bound by the Word of God to pray for the civil authorities, and *that's even more important than voting for them*! You will notice, by the way, as verses 3 and 4 show, that this command to pray for them comes in the context of God's desire that all men be saved and come to know the truth!

Questions and suggestions for thought or discussion

- Here are some questions that should engender thoughtful consideration and helpful discussion—but in all these matters a group discussion should be conducted without political heat (!) and in careful consideration of one another's views.

- In what ways does the government (at various levels) serve (or minister for) God?

- Is it OK to express criticism of a given government official? If so, what cautions should we observe in doing so?

- Will the application of these biblical passages be different for a Christian living in the United States, for example, from what it will be for a Christian living in, say, a dictatorship or in a country where the government is very corrupt? How?

- In what ways do you participate in the government's functions? Have you considered a larger role, and if so what? What are the pros and cons for Christians regarding holding elected or appointed office?

- What are some of the most pressing issues you think our government (at whatever level) faces? In what ways do you think Christians should involve themselves in such issues, and should this be merely as individuals or with the name and voice of the church?

- If you know someone who is a Christian and holds some government position, describe how you think that person does well in balancing his or her personal life with political responsibilities.

- Make it a point to learn what "civil religion" is, and then describe how we can avoid confusing the conduct and welfare of the state (or country) with that of God and the church.

- Do you pray for those in authority? If you do, consider telling others (especially if in a discussion group) just how you do this. If not, will you repent of this neglect and begin doing so? How can we go about this responsibility, and how should our church help us in this?

- Pick one of the concluding six observations, above, and think of some practical examples of how these observations will (or won't) work.

Chapter 8

Submissiveness in the Church

All Christians, aware of it or not, are intended by our Lord to be part of the life of a church—a local church. We are part of the Church universal, of course, but each local church is like a microcosm of that larger body, and it provides the context for Christian living.

A Place to Start: Ephesians 4:1-4

Important in understanding our relationship to a church is Ephesians 4:1-4. At the heart of this passage, Paul insists that we ought to be "endeavoring to keep the unity of the Spirit" (verse 3). That unity is the work of the Holy Spirit, who creates one body. When a person becomes a Christian, the Holy Spirit creates a bond between him or her and other believers. We are not left to "go it alone" in the Christian journey. We need one another. Our success as Christians, versus failure, under normal circumstances, requires the presence and help of other believers in a community of faith.

If the Holy Spirit creates and fosters this unity, it is our responsibility to keep—or guard or preserve—that unity. We can allow it to be damaged or broken, or we can keep it strong and healthy. And we are assured that if promoting this unity is the Spirit's concern and the object of His work within and among us, then we will not experience His fullness if we allow the fellowship to be fractured.

In a sense, then, we are on a journey together in the church, members of a spiritual family in pilgrimage, temporarily passing through a world that is not home, citizens of another country, as we saw in 1 Peter 1:17; 2:11. Just as submissiveness should characterize relationships in the nuclear family (next chapter), so it must in the spiritual family we belong to.

These four verses in Ephesians 5 make this clear. The very sentence that includes "endeavoring to keep the unity of the Spirit" introduces that duty with phrases that describe just what is required to fulfill it: "with all lowliness (humility) and gentleness (meekness), with longsuffering, bearing with one another in love" (verse 2). This is submissiveness expressed in a clear and uniquely appropriate way.

Lowliness (tapeinophrosunē) is humility, the very word we studied in chapter 1 in this volume. *Gentleness (prautēs)* is meekness, the word treated in chapter 2. As already noted, humility is seeing oneself as lowly and so seeing oneself rightly. Meekness follows immediately as the way humility expresses itself when the humble person is relating to God or others. Together the two qualities make up the very substance of *submissiveness*, of passing the time of our stay here in *fear* (1 Peter 1:17).

Here Paul associates these two powerful words with three others: longsuffering, forbearance, and love. *Longsuffering* (*makrothumia*) means keeping one's passions, especially anger, in check. *Forbearance* (expressed here by the verb *anechomai*) means holding oneself back, thus to bear with or endure. Here the idea seems to be to put up with others patiently. *Love* (*agapē*) is not mere emotion but a deliberate choosing to extend oneself on another's behalf.

What a challenging picture these five words paint together, like an artist's colors in a beautiful painting! Humility, meekness, longsuffering, forbearance, and love. By exercising these graces we can preserve the unity that the Holy Spirit has created. By exercising these graces we will necessarily promote submissiveness, each to the other, in the life of a church.

This is the picture that each reader should carry into all the rest of the discussion in this chapter.

Passages Requiring Mutual Submission in the Church

1. Consider Ephesians 5:21, "submitting to one another in the fear of God." I will use this as a key to understanding the family relationships described in Ephesians 5:22–6:9, dealt with in the following chapter. The verse certainly applies to both wives and husbands, both children and parents, both slaves and masters.

But the verse is even broader. It is directed to *all* of Paul's readers and applies to everyone in the Christian community. Indeed, verse 21 is the final part of a much longer sentence that extends back (at least) to verse 18. The whole sentence appeals to readers to be filled with the Holy Spirit (rather than being drunkards, verse 18), speaking to each other and to the Lord, from the heart, in the public singing in worship (verse 19), always expressing thanksgiving to God (verse 20), and mutually submitting to each other (verse 21). (There is no shortage of breathtaking pictures in this epistle!)

We learn much from this packed instruction. The corporate life of a church is affected by the fullness of the Holy Spirit, which is seen in the heartfelt music of the *congregation* (not performers!) assembled in worship, in their expressions of thanksgiving to God, and in their exchange of submissiveness, each to the other, demonstrated in attitude and observable actions. Without a full measure of this there will not be a full measure of the Holy Spirit in the life of a church or its members.

Do I need to say again? This is submissiveness actually demonstrated by every member of the congregation to every other member of the congregation.

2. Consider also 1 Peter 5:5b: "Yes, all of you be submissive to one another, and be clothed with humility, for 'God resists the proud, but gives grace to the humble.'" Perhaps Peter had been reading Paul! (See 2 Peter 3:15-16.) "All of you" means all his readers in several different churches, "the pilgrims of the Dispersion in Pontus, Galatia, Cappadocia, Asia, and Bithynia" in Asia Minor (1 Peter 1:1).

Peter is saying the very same thing Paul said. One can't miss the fact that he, too, links this directly to humility, as it must be. And, to back up his instruction, he quotes from Proverbs 3:34: "God resists the proud, but gives grace to the humble."

The first part of 1 Peter 5:5 calls for a specific manifestation of this mutual or reciprocal submission: "Likewise you younger people submit yourselves to your elders" (NKJV). There is some difference of opinion, among interpreters, about the precise nature of this admonition, the question being what *elders* Peter means. Does he mean older members of the congregation in general? Or, given that he has just laid down instructions to official "elders" in the church (verses 1-4), does he mean those officers specifically? The Greek original simply reads, "Likewise, younger (ones), be submitted to elders (or, older ones)." Even translations show different answers to this question, as in the following.

—"Ye younger, submit yourselves unto the elder" (KJV).

—"You who are younger, be subject to the elders" (ESV).

—"You who are younger, submit yourselves to your elders" (NIV).

—"You younger men, likewise, be subject to your elders" (NASB).

—"You younger men, follow the leadership of those who are older" (TLB).

—"You younger men must submit yourselves to the older men" (TEV).

In all this variety there are three different ways of treating the word *elders.* (1) Some add a "the" and take it to mean the officers of the church who have that status. (2) Some take it to mean, simply, older people in comparison to younger ones and translate with "older." (3) Others make no decision and render it "your elders," which can be taken either way. Anyone who reads several commentaries on the passage will find the same differences of opinion.

If this means the official church elders, then the verse belongs in the same category as will be discussed in a subsequent section of this chapter. If it means, more generally, that the younger people in the church should demonstrate submissiveness toward those who are older, then that is a special application of the principle of mutual submission for the younger members as they relate to older ones.

The latter is certainly a valid application, given that respect for the elderly—considering their age (or length of time as believers) and experience—should be part of church life. In favor of this view of the verse is the fact that a definite article ("the") is not used with either substantival adjective ("younger," "older/elder") in the original, supporting the idea that younger ones should show submission or subjection to older ones. Furthermore, if the official elders were meant, then all the congregation should manifest submission to them and not just younger members.[18]

Some Practical Manifestations of Submissiveness in Church Life

Regardless of the particular clause just discussed, both inspired apostles—Paul and Peter—require all believers in a church to practice mutual submission, each one submitting to every other one. Neither apostle tells us fully *how* that will look, but there is a

---

[18] Bo Reike, *The Epistles of James, Peter, and Jude*, in the *Anchor Bible* (Garden City, NY: Doubleday, 1964) 139, in support of such a view, takes the "younger" to mean "junior" and to "represent the rest of the congregation." This does not seem likely.

great deal in the New Testament that will lead to practical applications of this principle. Consider the following.

One important manifestation of this submission is developed in 1 Corinthians 8-10 and Romans 14-15. Those who have a well-developed sense of liberty in debated matters must not declare their independence from those who are "weaker" in such things. Submissiveness means considering the weaker brother's spiritual welfare and governing one's liberty in accord with that consideration.

Galatians 5:13 speaks about our mutual submissiveness: "For you, brethren, have been called to liberty, only do not use liberty as an opportunity for the flesh, but through love serve one another." In that context, the liberty referred to is freedom from the requirements of the Mosaic Law (like circumcision) for one's salvation. We must stand fast in that liberty (5:1), but we must not permit our sense of liberty to lead us into the indulgence of sinful flesh or indifference to the spiritual welfare of others. Our love for others may well lead us to limit the exercise of our liberty in order to foster mutual service. *Serve*, here (*douleuō*) is a strong word, referring to the bond-service rendered by a slave. Serving one another, ministering to each other's needs, is one way submission expresses itself.

Galatians 6 mentions several ways submission in church life will stand out. For example, if one member falls into sin, others will restore him to spiritual health "in a spirit of gentleness": that is, *meekness* (verse 1)—which includes being conscious of one's own vulnerability. Another example is in verse 2: "Bear one another's burdens." While there are some responsibilities that each person must carry before God alone (verse 5),[19] believers often have difficulties to bear and their companions in Christ ought to bear those with them. That requires submissiveness.

Ephesians 4:32 contributes to developing this theme: "Be kind to one another, tender-hearted, forgiving one another, even as God in Christ forgave you." Showing kindness, compassion, and forgiveness to each other is an important way we demonstrate mutual submission in the life of the church. And why shouldn't we do this? As Paul reminds us pointedly, God has shown kindness, compassion, and forgiveness to us!

Consider Philippians 2:4: "Let each of you look out not only for his own interests, but also for the interests of others." Paul illustrates this with the example of Christ Himself, who gave up Heaven to become a servant among us and experience shameful death for us. There has never been a stronger example of submissiveness than this, and we are expected to emulate and model the same self-sacrificing submissiveness in devoting ourselves to the well-being of our fellow followers of Jesus.

Similarly, Colossians 3:12-13 speaks eloquently about this mutual submissiveness and ties it up in a single passage with humility and meekness and some other equally powerful words: "Therefore, as the elect of God, holy and beloved, put on tender mercies, kindness, humility, meekness, longsuffering, bearing with one another, and forgiving one another, if anyone has a complaint against another, even as Christ forgave you, so you also must do."

---

[19] *Burdens* in verse 3 and *burden* in verse 5 are two different Greek words.

I could add at least as many more passages that describe what submissiveness will look like in actual practice within the life of a church. The reader can surely find many such passages. Mutual submissiveness in the church morphs into lots of beautiful things practiced reciprocally: serving, tolerating, forgiving, restoring, encouraging, helping, teaching, worshipping, bearing, supporting, and giving. And that's not a complete list.

Submission to Church's Leaders

One of the special matters of submissiveness in church life involves submission to its chosen leaders. The New Testament has much to say about this, and I will comment on key passages, first providing a brief survey of basic biblical material on the subject.

Very early, the new Christian churches (assemblies, congregations) chose *elders* (Acts 14:23; cf. 20:17), apparently following the pattern of synagogue life that Jewish Christians were already familiar with. Even earlier, on at least one occasion, a specific need led to the selection of seven men to supervise distributions to needy widows (Acts 6:1-6). Whether those were the first deacons or not, it is clear that there were soon *pastors* (or *bishops*) and *deacons* in the churches, since Paul provides qualifications for them (1 Timothy 3:1-13) and includes them in his opening address in Philippians (1:1). I think it likely that our modern pastor and deacons correspond to the early elders, but that view—not held by many other interpreters—isn't essential to the purpose of this discussion. For that matter, with our contemporary (plural) pastoral staffs, we have developed even beyond that.

Whatever the structure and titles, it is biblical for the church to identify leaders. And the New Testament material that describes the church's relationship to its leaders doesn't focus on titles but on function. Here are two key descriptions.

1. Hebrews 13 refers to the church leaders, and to the church's relationship to them, three times.

—Verse 7: "Remember *those who rule over you*, who have spoken the word of God to you, whose faith follow, considering the outcome of their conduct."

—Verse 17: "Obey *those who rule over you*, and be submissive, for they watch out for your souls, as those who must give account. Let them do so with joy and not with grief, for that would be unprofitable for you."

—Verse 24: "Greet all *those who rule over you*."

In all three verses, "those who rule over you" means the same as "the ones leading you," using a verb (*hēgeomai*) which means to lead, guide, or rule over and can be used very broadly in a general way or narrowly in a specific way. But it refers to a role or activity—a *function*, in other words—and does not identify a specific office. Perhaps this would have included elders, as well as "bishops and deacons," in the early churches, but it might have included more.

Regardless of title, these leaders did at least three things: (1) they ministered the Word of God to the church (verse 7); (2) they set an example in the practice of the Christian faith for the church (verse 7); and (3) they watched out for the welfare of the souls of those in the church (verse 17). They were leaders, indeed, with heavy responsibilities.

At any rate, other than giving these leaders the writer's greetings (verse 24), the readers of Hebrews were instructed, first, to *remember* them (verse 7). The practical implications of this are left to us to fill in; as one Greek lexicon says, the word as it is used here has "no fixed boundaries."[20] The basic idea is to have them in mind, and this no doubt implies a number of different things, based on being conscious that they have leadership responsibility. Thus one will "remember" them in recognition and respect, in praying for them, and in supporting them—and in other ways.

I pause long enough to fill in some of the space involved in the word *support*. Galatians 6:6 instructs the one who is taught the word of God to "share in all good things" with the one who teaches. First Timothy 5:17 exhorts, "Let the elders who rule well be counted worthy of double honor, especially those who labor in the word and doctrine (or teaching)." Here *rule* is a different word (*prohistēmi*), which literally means "to stand before"—as a leader, of course. Many interpreters take this "double honor" to include their financial support, and I tend to think they are right in this. Regardless, appropriate honor or recognition includes support. Consider the decree of Jesus Himself, "Even so the Lord has commanded that those who preach the gospel should live from the gospel" (1 Corinthians 9:14). Even this financial support is a manifestation of submissiveness when one contributes from his own substance to free the pastor-teacher to minister the word.

---

[20] Arndt, William F., and Gingrich, F. Wilbur, *A Greek-English Lexicon of the New Testament and Other Early Christian Literature* (Chicago: University of Chicago Press, 1957) 526.

Not only are we to remember or recognize the leaders, we are also to follow the example of their faith. As they model a life of faith in accord with the teaching of Jesus and the apostles, so those under their leadership or watch-care should live by the same example (verse 7b). Saving faith, by the way, is always "lived out." Indeed, the writer of Hebrews instructs the readers to consider the outcome of the leaders' conduct, or their lived-out faith, and that outcome is defined in terms of their eternal destiny. Verse 7 is apparently looking primarily to some leaders who have already gone on to their eternal reward.

Still another duty the writer places on his readers concerning their leaders: *obey* them, specifically manifesting submissiveness (verse 17). The word translated *obey* (*peithomai*) is, literally, *be persuaded by*, and *be submissive* is not the word I have commented on before (*hupotassō*). This one (*hupeikō*) means, literally, to yield or submit to authority, which matches the idea of obedience. They are to listen in order to be taught, and then they are to submit by embracing what they learned in practice. This is submissiveness in a specific form, a voluntary compliance with the leaders' teachings that are rightly grounded in the Scriptures.

Verse 17 provides a rich context for this requirement, exposing three things involved. (1) The leaders are responsible to watch for the souls of those under their charge. That is serious business, indeed, when the welfare of one's eternal self is at stake. (2) The leaders must "give account"—to the Lord, that is. They will stand before Him and make a report and be evaluated and rewarded—or not—accordingly. (3) The leaders ought to be able to carry out their ministry with joy and not in grief, and the submissiveness of their followers plays a large role in determining this. Resistance causes them grief, following their model and teaching brings them joy.

2. First Thessalonians 5:12-13 also presents a persuasive picture of the role of leaders and requires the submissiveness of those in the church under their leadership.

> [12] And we urge you, brethren, to recognize those who labor among you, and are over you in the Lord and admonish you, [13] and to esteem them very highly in love for their work's sake. Be at peace among yourselves.

The meaning of this instruction is easily uncovered by treating (1) the responsibilities of the leaders and (2) the responsibilities of those in the church.

The leaders do three things. (1) They "labor among you," where the word labor (*kopiaō*) suggests the kind of work that may well tire one out. The point is that their work isn't easy; the responsibility is heavy. (2) They "are over you in the Lord." The word used here is the same as in 1 Timothy 5:17 and means *stand before*. In other words, they are "up front" as leaders. (See also Romans 12:8, where the word occurs again.) Like the usage in Hebrews 13, this also refers to function and not to a specific office. (3) They "admonish you." This word (*noutheteō*) suggests "putting in mind" and refers to instruction, often carrying with it the implication of admonition or warning. All this—the toiling, leading, and instructing—comprises the "work" (verse 13) they do and which all of us must submit to.

Those in the church have two duties to fulfill. (1) They are to "recognize" the leaders as such. This word (*oida*) literally means to *know* and so to recognize or acknowledge them for the leadership role and responsibility they have. The words are different, but the meaning is close to that of *remember* in Hebrews 13:7, quoted and discussed above. (2) They are likewise to "esteem them highly in love." *Esteem* (*hēgeomai*) means to count or regard, and the strong adverb *highly* (*huperekperissou*) might well be rendered as *most highly* or *to the highest degree*. This closely matches the honor, perhaps even the "double honor" that Paul enjoins in 1 Timothy 5:17 (above).

Everything about this passage bespeaks submissiveness to the church's leaders. They have been placed—under God's leadership, one trusts—in a position of heavy responsibility and (at least until they disqualify themselves) ought to be highly respected, followed, and supported. Here in 1 Thessalonians, Paul immediately attaches an important admonition, one that will result when leaders carry out their responsibilities faithfully and members honor them in "follow-ship," honor, and support; peace within the congregation will surely prevail.

Conclusion

No doubt other implications of submissiveness in church life could be brought out, like the occasional need for submission to church discipline, for example. One verse already mentioned, Galatians 6:1, touches on this when it urges those who are spiritually minded—and thus mature—to restore a member who has fallen into sin. In that case, Paul observes that the one doing the restoring must act with meekness, and the person will be restored successfully only if he or she submits to and meekly accepts the labor and admonition. Jesus laid the foundation for church discipline in

Matthew 18:15-20, and two specific instances of church discipline are explained in 1 Corinthians 5 and 2 Thessalonians 3:6-15. As is true in Galatians 6:1, both the church and the member being disciplined should act in humility and meekness and so preserve the unity of the church and the spiritual well-being of every member.

Again, then, submissiveness in the life of a church is *reciprocal*, each manifesting subjection to the other in a mutual commitment to serve one another. Even the leaders are servant leaders and submit their self-interest to that of the members they serve in the spirit of Philippians 2:4.

Our Free Will Baptist Church Covenant begins, "Having given ourselves to God … we now give ourselves to one another." The fifth paragraph is a winsome example of what this means:

We agree to accept Christian admonition and reproof with meekness, and to watch over one another in love, endeavoring to "keep the unity of the Spirit" in the bonds of peace, to be careful of one another's happiness and reputation, and seek to strengthen the weak, encourage the afflicted, admonish the erring, and so far as we are able to promote the success of the church and the Gospel.

Let us strive to ensure, by our mutual submission to each other in the life of the church, that this is our reality.

Questions and suggestions for thought or discussion

- Name some of the offices/officers in the church that you should show submission toward. Now identify (in writing or mentally) all the ways you can think of that you and other church members should demonstrate submissiveness toward them.

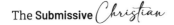

- If an officer of the church (or any member, for that matter) has acted wrongly in a way that is public or known by more people than yourself, how should you go about seeking their acknowledgment of wrongdoing?

- If anyone in the church (including yourself!) violates the standards of church behavior, how should that person be dealt with? Discuss what is required of both the offender and anyone who attempts to rectify the situation. In what way(s) is submissiveness required on both sides?

- Are you among the younger or the older members of your church? What are some ways each of these should manifest a submissive spirit to the other?

- Are you an officer—pastor, deacon, whatever—in your church? What are some ways reciprocal submission will affect you so that you demonstrate submissiveness? How does what is called "servant leadership" come into play here?

- Pick one of the New Testament passages discussed in this chapter. Suggest more implications of it for life in your church than just those mentioned in the chapter.

- Are there any specific issues within the membership of your church where the principles of 1 Corinthians 8-10 and Romans 13-14—when so-called "stronger" Christians should consider limiting their liberty for so-called "weaker" ones? If so, what are they and how might any possible tension or harm be avoided?

- Read the Free Will Baptist Church Covenant and identify any matters mentioned there that may require submissiveness on the part of church members.

Chapter 9

Submissiveness in the Family Circle

This chapter deals with the way Christians manifest submissiveness in family relationships. I will pursue this primarily as an exposition of Ephesians 5:21–6:9, supplementing it with other passages in the New Testament that provide additional detail.

One should realize, in approaching these passages, that they express application of the principles *within the cultural context of the time.* The believers addressed in the New Testament letters by inspired apostles did not live in a vacuum, and the letters themselves expose the home context they lived in.

Briefly, there could be three pairs of inhabitants in a home in the New Testament world, with somewhat different roles: (1) wives and husbands; (2) children and their parents; and (3) servants or slaves and their masters. This is the way Paul pursues the discussion, both in Ephesians and in the parallel passage in Colossians 3:18–4:1. One can't miss the fact that in treating each of the three pairs he addresses the more subservient member first—

wives, children, slaves—and the one regarded in their culture as having the greater authority last—husbands, parents, masters.

But there is an important principle up front that speaks directly to both sides in each pair.[21]

Ephesians 5:21, Standing Over the Entire Passage

It is important not to miss this. The sentence that leads directly to the passage (5:22–6:9) ends with the words "submitting to one another in the fear of God," which I treated in the previous chapter but desire to focus on again. *Submitting* and *fear* are two of the four words I have focused on in the earlier chapters and so are of primary importance for the exposition of this passage.

This sentence covers verses 18-21, which expands on the meaning of being Spirit-filled as expressing itself in three ways (in participles): (1) *speaking* to each other in the church's music (verse 19), (2) *giving thanks* to God always (verse 20), and (3) *submitting* to each other (verse 21). It would be equally possible to take the third participle as equivalent to a new imperative that starts a new sentence. Whether we do this or not, it is clear that verse 22 and the rest of the passage to follow expands on the practical meaning of submitting to one another.

Before we pass on to that expansion, however, we ought to stop here long enough to emphasize that verse 21 speaks of all aspects of life within the church, the community of followers of

---

[21] Since today's family does not include slaves, I will deal with the slave-master relationship in another chapter devoted to employment.

Christ. Submission or subjection to each other as fellow believers should characterize everyone in the church and be manifested in submitting one's individual (*self*-ish) concerns to the welfare of every other believer in the church. That has been the topic of the preceding chapter. In this chapter, the point is that the same basic attitude of mutual or reciprocal submission applies equally to the nuclear family.

Wives and Husbands (Ephesians 5:22-33)

1. The *wives* are addressed first, briefly (verses 22-24, 33b).

> [22] Wives, submit to your own husbands, as to the Lord.
> [23] For the husband is head of the wife, as also Christ is head of the church; and He is the Savior of the body. [24] Therefore, just as the church is subject to Christ, so *let* the wives *be* to their own husbands in everything.…
> [33b] and let the wife see that she respects her husband.

There is but one command here: namely, for Christian wives to be in respectful submission to their husbands. *Submit* (verse 22) and *be subject to* (verse 24) translate the very same Greek verb (*hupotassomai*), which is the specific verb used in verse 21. They mean exactly the same thing. The verb *respect* in verse 33b is different, being the same as is usually translated *fear* (*phobeō*). No doubt *respect* is justified as a translation, but it has the full meaning that we have seen in our study of the word in 1 Peter (chapter 3).

Paul provides grounds for the command in verses 23-24: namely, that the Christian wife knows her husband is her *head* and is submissive for that reason, just as the church as a whole is submissive to Christ as its head. I will not attempt to summarize all the discussion that has gone on in Christian circles over the meaning of *head* (*kephalē*). One should arrive at the practical meaning from the analogy Paul draws, comparing the wife-husband relationship to the church-Christ relationship. Regardless, the relationship is marked by submissiveness on the part of the church to Christ and on the part of the wife to her husband.

The parallel passage in Colossians 3:18 is much briefer and adds no content except to say that the wife's submission is "fitting in the Lord": that is, the submission is appropriate or proper in view of and in the realm of their common bond in union with Jesus Christ as Lord of them both.

First Peter 3:1-7 also speaks to Christian husbands and wives, and the first six verses address the wives in a way that is very similar to that of Paul here in Ephesians. But Peter adds a unique consideration, applying this submissiveness even in the case of Christian wives whose husbands were unbelievers. In such a case, the submission will often manifest itself in resisting the impulse to "preach" to the husband and choosing, instead, to focus on the wife's own conduct as a way to win him to faith. In that case, she should concentrate on: (1) *chaste conduct*, which is purity in action; (2) *fear*, which is submissiveness (as discussed in the chapter on 1 Peter); (3) *cultivating inner beauty* rather than focusing primarily on outward, cosmetic concerns—which does not justify indifference to appearance; and (4) *following the example of godly women* in the Bible (like Sarah) who manifested submission to their husbands.

Having said all that, the temptation for me now is to jump immediately into practical application, expounding what it means for Christian wives to be submissive to their husbands. But I think it can be dangerous to do this without first analyzing what the inspired text says to husbands. After that discussion we can be more well-rounded in discerning how Paul's teaching should be put into practice, within the home, by both wives and husbands.

2. The husbands are addressed next, and more extensively (Ephesians 5:25-33a).

> [25] Husbands, love your wives, just as Christ also loved the church and gave Himself for her, [26] that He might sanctify and cleanse her with the washing of water by the word, [27] that He might present her to Himself a glorious church, not having spot or wrinkle or any such thing, but that she should be holy and without blemish.

We will come back to verses 28-33 shortly.

Where the appeal to wives is for subjection, the appeal to husbands is for love. The interpreter, however, should never think that this is an absolute distinction, with only one of the two appeals for wives and only one for husbands. The best way to see this is to ask oneself whether wives are not to love their husbands, and the answer is, of course they are. Then the same logic may well apply to the other side of the equation: are husbands to be in subjection to their wives? The answer to this is also yes. See this first in what I have already said about verse 21, which stands over the whole passage: the submission is *mutual*: wives and husbands to each other.

Even more important, see this in the appeal to love. For one thing, consider that *love,* in the Bible (New Testament, *agapaō*) does not refer to mere emotion. The word speaks of volition and action, depicting a deliberate choice on behalf of another's welfare. And Paul leaves us no doubt about how strong this is; husbands are to love their wives *as Christ loved the church.*

How did Christ love the church? He "gave Himself for it." In other words, His love was *self-sacrificing,* as Christian love always is. This appeal is nothing more or less than what Jesus commanded in John 15:12-13: "This is My commandment, that you love one another as I have loved you. Greater love has no one than this, than to lay down one's life for his friends."

In other words, this love is submissiveness in the highest degree, sacrificing one's own interests—yes, even one's life—for the sake of the object of one's love. Self-sacrifice is exactly what is meant by submissiveness, even when we can correctly call it love.

The parallel passage in Colossians 3:19 is briefer, adding only that the husband must not be "bitter" (*pikrainō*) toward his wife. The precise meaning of the word is argued by interpreters; some suggest *harsh* and others *incensed* or *angry.* Either attitude would not be a manifestation of self-sacrificing love.

First Peter 3:7 also adds interesting contextual elements to the discussion. As I have noted in the chapter on 1 Peter, the "likewise" places husbands, like wives, under the requirement of submissiveness. In summary, Peter instructs Christian husbands to *understand* and *honor* their wives. This will entail taking cognizance of the fact that they are "weaker vessels" and "fellow-heirs" of the grace of eternal life—thus recognizing their status in both the natural and the spiritual realms. On the one hand, they are weaker physically and (often) socio-economically. On the other, they are equally gifted with God's saving grace. The Christian husband then, in self-sacrificing love, deliberately chooses to put his wife in the place of honor in the family circle.

Especially helpful is the way Paul has in view, throughout this lesson on the husband-wife relationship, the relationship between Christ and His church. Thus the wife submits to her husband as the church submits to Christ (verse 24), and the husband loves his wife as Christ loves the church (verse 25). Ephesians 5:28-33 develops the analogy between wives/husbands and the church/Christ in even more detail. Just as the biblical provision for marriage, from its Genesis beginning, represents a man and his wife as "one flesh," so Christ and the church are one body. The church is thus the body of Christ, and the wife by analogy the body of her husband. The self-sacrifice, then, is mutual. So is the submissiveness.

We need to read the Ephesians passage on two levels, then. At one level, the wife and husband are both meant to demonstrate self-sacrificing love for each other and to manifest submission toward each other. At another level, the inspired Paul speaks *especially* of the wife's submission and of the husband's love. This raises the question whether there is any intentional difference in roles and in the form submission and love take in those two roles.

The answer, apparently, is that some difference is intentional, and the grounds for this seems clearly to lie in the fact that "the husband is head of the wife, as also Christ is head of the church" (verse 23). If it were not for that statement, we might easily regard everything said in this passage as requiring exactly equal and mutual submission and love on both sides of the husband-wife relationship. But the observation is here, and it is inspired, and we can't afford to ignore it.

This is where a great deal of fairly recent discussion about the meaning and implications of headship comes in, a discussion I will not even attempt to summarize. It is enough, for now, to focus on the analogy between Christ and the church that Paul himself uses as a basis for speaking of headship. Christ's headship in the body that is composed of Himself and the church lies in the fact that He loves it (verse 25), is its Savior (verse 23), gave Himself for it (verse 25), washed, sanctified, and cleansed it (verse 26) in order to bring it to Himself in purity and holiness (verse 27), and nourishes and cherishes it (verse 28).

What a marvelous picture of "headship"! I am persuaded that if husbands manifest such headship their wives will have little trouble manifesting submission. Do I mean to suggest that there is no *authority* involved in such headship? No, but I would emphasize that whatever authority this headship carries is fully *earned* by the self-sacrificing love of the husband who takes seriously the demands that fell on Christ as a result of His love for the church. I will say more about the form this will take, in principle, in the application section to follow.

Application: Christian Wives and Husbands

I am a great believer in the fact that the Bible teaches the people of God to live by *principles* more than by detailed regulations.

Of course, there are some clearly-expressed dos and don'ts, like explicit prohibitions against murder, adultery, theft, and lying. But most of what we're expected to live by is presented in principles that apply broadly across a fairly wide spectrum of behavior. This approach doesn't "let us off the hook." To the contrary, it becomes our responsibility, maturely, to determine what those principles are and how to put them into practice in a variety of situations.

I see three principles, at least, in the discussion, above, regarding the teaching of Ephesians 5 (and other passages) relating to the wife-husband relationship for Christians. (1) Both husbands and wives—and perhaps especially husbands—are to love their spouses with a self-sacrificing love modeled after that of Christ for His church. (2) Both husbands and wives—and perhaps especially wives—are to demonstrate submission to their spouses, a submission that also involves self-sacrifice and is modeled after the church's submission to Christ. (3) The husband has a headship role that is modeled after the headship of Christ over His church, and a wife is obligated to honor this in her attitudes and behavior.

So what will these principles look like in actual practice? This is something each individual must figure out for himself or herself, *provided he or she grapples seriously with the principles* and makes a conscientious attempt to determine just how to live them out. I will not try to posit specific regulations that Christians should follow, but I will offer a few suggestions as to how to go about applying the principles—first for husbands and then for wives.

Ideally, the Christian husband will be guided by the dual principles of submission and self-sacrificing love, recognizing that both are mutual. He will also recognize that his headship responsibility requires that he is to be the savior, protector, provider, cleanser, nourisher, and cherisher of his wife. That he gives himself for her means he sacrifices selfish concerns to put her welfare—physical, spiritual, and emotional—at the top of his family priorities. He may be called on to die for her, as Jesus was. Even if he is not, he will be called on to sacrifice time, energy, money, and other things he holds dear for her. He will give anything he can to purify and sanctify her to himself, and that quest includes an unrelenting commitment of himself to her and her alone.

The husband's headship is at least as much a matter of responsibility as authority. To the degree that there is authority involved, he may well be the one to make final decisions at times; but he will not do so without full consideration for her needs and opinions. He will put her well-being first. He will not be a dictator or harsh.

Ideally, the Christian wife will also be guided by the same dual principles of mutual submission and self-sacrificing love. She too will sacrifice her self-interests for the welfare of her husband, which will require time and energy and other things she holds dear. She will recognize her husband's headship, and this will occasionally mean submitting to his final decisions. But the relationship is not a servile one, and her submission—like his—is given freely in love. I find it interesting that in both of the other pairs of family relationships Paul treats in this passage—children and parents, slaves and masters—*obedience* is required of the more subservient member (children, 6:1; slaves, 6:5). Not so with the wives, even though being in subjection isn't far removed from that in various circumstances.

Each husband and wife will love, trust, and support the other.

Children and Parents (Ephesians 6:1-4)

1. The *children* are addressed first (verses 1-3).

> [1]Children, obey your parents in the Lord, for this is right.
> [2]"Honor your father and mother," which is the first com-
> mandment with promise: [3]"that it may be well with you
> and you may live long on the earth."

The passage assumes these are children still living at home under
their parents' watch-care. (I will comment below on how the relationship changes later in life.)

Two things are required of children at home toward their parents: *honor* (as in the fifth commandment, Exodus 20:12; Deuteronomy 5:16), and *obedience*, which is one way honoring parents
expresses itself. To *obey* (*hupakouō*) literally means to hearken or
to listen submissively. The parallel passage in Colossians 3:20 uses
the same word. That this is "in the Lord" indicates the basis of the
relationship in the Christian family; they are in union, together, in
Christ and His authority lies behind the commanded obedience—
in the same way that God's authority lies behind our commanded
obedience of civil authorities.

To *honor* (*timaō*) is broader and includes obedience. It means
to show them respect in attitude, speech, and behavior.

What about when children are grown and gone from the
home? While detailed obedience is no longer required, giving
honor is. This means that adult children must still show respect
and care for their parents, making sure they are well provided for.

In other words, the requirement of mutual submissiveness in
5:21, which stands over the entire passage, is still in force. And

Paul provides two reasons for this. First, this is right, both for the child-parent relationship and for obedience to the command of God. Second, a promise attaches to the fifth commandment. Originally, its primary meaning was probably that the Israelite community would enjoy longevity in the Land of Promise if family life was characterized by obedient children. By practical extension, the promise probably includes a general (not absolute) expectation that obedient children will tend to live longer because they observe their parents' instructions for their own well-being. Colossians 3:20 adds a third reason, although it is implied in the first two: namely, obedience and honor for one's parents—submissiveness, in other words—will please God.

2. Parents are addressed next (verse 4).

> ⁴And you, fathers, do not provoke your children to wrath, but bring them up in the training and admonition of the Lord.

As in Hebrews 11:23, *fathers* probably means *parents*. They have a negative and positive responsibility to their children, and even in this role they are exercising submission toward those under their authority at home; verse 5:21 is still in effect. To carry out these responsibilities will also require self-sacrificing love, demanding time and energy devoted to the well-being of their children.

On the negative side, they are not to provoke their children's wrath, which Colossians 3:21 explains may lead to their being discouraged. I assume Paul means a provocation that is uncalled for, one that arises from inconsistent or unreasonable demands or discipline. Such demands or discipline can easily arise from a one-sided concern to please oneself rather than a carefully considered action for the benefit of the child. Children who live under unreasonable or inconsistent expectations can become defeated in such a way that they are negatively affected for life. Parents who indulge their selfish inclinations in dealing with their children can foster such intimidation.

On the positive side, the parental responsibility is expressed as one primary responsibility that includes three words: *bring them up*, *training*, and *admonition*. The first of these is the very same word (*ektrephō*) that was translated *nourishes* in 5:29; this is apparently the main requirement, which the other two words develop. Like husbands toward their wives, then, the parents' goal is to provide for their children's true needs and to nurture their development as whole persons. Again, this requires self-sacrificing love and submission on the part of the parents.

The *training* (*paideia*) is a word often meaning chastisement or discipline, but it is as much positive as negative and refers to the entire program used in rearing children. This will include giving children right direction as well as correcting misbehavior. All of this is *discipline* in the broader sense, and in that sense the word would be a good translation here.

Admonition (*nouthesia*) is, literally, "putting in mind." It means instruction in the right way and usually carries with it the idea of instruction fortified by warning. The phrase "of the Lord" probably goes with both words and indicates that the ways taught are the ways of the Lord. This entire, short paragraph is wrapped in the consciousness that these are the ways of *Christians* and reflect their relationship to the Lord and the desire that both the parents and the children walk in His ways.

Once again, Paul has given us *principles* and expects us to take them seriously and determine the best ways to apply those principles in parenting and in what we teach and expect of our children. Again, too, both children and parents are to manifest the *substance* of submissiveness in their responsibilities toward the other, even though the *form* which this submissiveness will take will be different in the two roles.

I will not treat the slave-master relationship in this lesson, since that is not part of family life in our circumstances. The next lesson, however, will make use of the passages that speak to that relationship.

Conclusion

Having just used the word *form*, I want to suggest the practical benefit of distinguishing between *form* and *substance*—a distinction I first encountered long ago as used by my friend and colleague Leroy Forlines. The *substance* of anything is what's at the essence or heart of it, the element that's always there regardless of the circumstances or situation. The *form*, however, can be different from one time and place to another, from one situation to another in which the substance is present.

That's the way things are with *submissiveness* (humility and meekness). The essence or substance of submissiveness remains the same in every circumstance, but the forms it takes will vary widely, depending on the circumstances and the roles people have. Both husbands and wives are required to be submissive to their mates, but the particular form that submissiveness takes may differ at times. In the family's life together, the wife's submissiveness may take the form of yielding to the requirements of the husband's work schedule, for example. The husband's submissiveness may take the form of sacrificing his desire to trade cars in light of his wife's desire for some home remodeling. But these are mere examples of possibilities; wives and husbands have to figure these things out in their own way. What's necessary is that both, in love and submission, seek the welfare of the other and sacrifice their own desires accordingly.

The same is true for children and parents. For the child at home, submissiveness may take the form of obeying a parent's rules, including those that the child finds impossible to understand. A parent's submissiveness may take the form of making time to attend the child's game or giving up buying a new suit or dress in order to give the child something he or she strongly desires. Again, these are possible examples; real life isn't always quite so obvious.

In other words, no matter how "egalitarian" one is, people's roles differ. Submissiveness will show itself in varied forms in varied roles. In an online article for *Christianity Today*, some time ago, I ran across a statement by Kyle Worley: "He, who possessed everything by right, surrendered it all for love." [22] For Jesus, the demand of love, namely to sacrifice Himself, outweighed the joy of possessing all things.

---

[22] Worley, Kyle, *Christianity Today*, "Why It's Easier to Accept David as a Murderer than a Rapist" (October 14, 2019). https://www.christianitytoday.com/ct/2019/october-web-only/david-bathsheba-debate-murder-rapist.html

A TV commercial airing before Christmas, both in 2020 and in 2021, showed a husband who had bought two new GMC trucks, one for himself and one for his wife. He meant the red one for her, but she immediately latched on to the green one; "I love it," she said. He paused a moment, then said, "I like red."

Questions and suggestions for thought or discussion

- How does love involve submissiveness?
- If you're a husband, name some ways you ought to be submissive, or show love, to your wife.
- If you're a wife, name some ways you ought to be submissive, or show love, to your husband.
- Do you agree that wives won't mind being in submission to their husbands if the husbands love them as Christ loved the church?
- How does a husband "give himself" for his wife?
- What are some of the differences between a child's responsibilities toward parents while still at home and, later on, when living in a place of his or her own?
- Whether to be shared with others or not, make a list of specific ways, in your home, that you should show submissiveness to your wife or husband or parents or children.
- Of the four groups in the family that are named, here, which one do you think has the greater difficulty showing submissiveness? Why?

Chapter 10

Submissiveness in the Workplace

In the previous chapter, I have dealt with the way Christian submissiveness manifests itself in the family circle. For homes in the world of the New Testament that circle could include slaves, who were completely subject to their masters. Consequently, New Testament discussion of family relationships often includes the role of slaves, as seen in Ephesians 5:22–6:9 (6:5-9) and Colossians 3:18–4:1 (3:22-4:1). But since our present households have no slaves in their structure, it seems better to use the *principles* regarding slaves and masters in a discussion of the workplace.

That is the approach I am taking. First I will, relatively briefly, analyze the passages that speak directly to slaves and masters, and in that way I will be continuing the treatment of Ephesians 5:21–6:9 begun in the previous chapter. After this analysis I will discuss the application in our workaday world. Christian submissiveness has important implications for us in that important part of our lives.

Before I do these two things, however, it should prove helpful to devote a short section to the matter of slavery in the world of the New Testament, focusing on the way Christians were expected to deal with that institution. Even in that there is a lesson about submissiveness.

Christians and Slavery in the New Testament

The New Testament was written for Christians in the Roman Empire during the first century A.D., although of course it was intended for Christians at any time and place. As I have already said, those who first received and read the Gospels and the Epistles lived in a context, and an important part of that context was defined by the Romans.

In that world slavery was common. There were millions of slaves and former slaves; the latter were "freedmen." Many became slaves as prisoners of war. A wealthy man might have a hundred, or even a thousand slaves, all considered part of his "household." Slavery might not always have been as oppressive as that which characterized the American South before the Civil War, but a slave was entirely at the disposal of his or her owner.

Some slave-holders were cruel; Peter forthrightly notes that some were "good and gentle," while others were "harsh" and might beat their slaves without justification (1 Peter 2:18-21). A slave might be scourged or mutilated or even executed at the master's will, although in the Roman social and legal structures there were some widely-held standards for the treatment of slaves. In some cases, slavery resulted in the improvement of the slave's circumstances in life, especially if that person had been in poverty before. Many slaves were well educated and given trusted management responsibilities. Those who were faithful and industrious might well expect to win their freedom, often within seven years.

It is not surprising, then, that there are numerous references, directly or indirectly, to slavery in the New Testament. What seems most interesting about these is the fact that Christians are not instructed, there, to go out and overthrow the institution of slavery. I would not want to be misunderstood for saying that. I have no doubt that the principles taught in the New Testament ultimately led to the abolishment of slavery where the Christian Scriptures are influential. Christianity ultimately overturns social injustice, even if it does not rise up in arms for a direct attack. But the immediate approach of the New Testament is to instruct Christians how to be Christians, in whatever circumstances they find themselves in the social order.

This is where submissiveness enters the picture. The Christian slave, caught in a set of circumstances approved in the social order and upheld by the government, is taught how to live and follow the example of Christ in that set of circumstances. Consequently, the inspired writers of the New Testament taught Christian slaves about submissiveness.[23]

---

[23] For some treatment of slavery in the New Testament world, see Arthur Rupprecht, "Christianity and the Slavery Question," *Bulletin of the Evangelical Theological Society* 6:2 (May 1963) 64–68; Edwin Yamauchi, "Slaves of God," *Bulletin of the Evangelical Theological Society* 9.1 (Winter 1966) 31–49.

Submissiveness for Slaves and Masters in Ephesians 6:5-9

Just as Paul addressed wives and husbands, children and parents, about submissiveness on both sides of these equations (previous chapter), so he addressed Christian slaves and their masters in the same context of family and with the same focus on submissiveness. We should remember that Ephesians 5:21, with its appeal for mutual submission, stands over all the instruction that continues from 5:20 through 6:9.

1. Paul addresses the Christian slaves first, in verses 5-8:

> [5] Bondservants, be obedient to those who are your masters according to the flesh, with fear and trembling, in sincerity of heart, as to Christ; [6] not with eyeservice, as men-pleasers, but as bondservants of Christ, doing the will of God from the heart, [7] with goodwill doing service, as to the Lord, and not to men, [8] knowing that whatever good anyone does, he will receive the same from the Lord, whether *he is* a slave or free.

This is one sentence and it contains just one imperative verb, "be obedient" (verse 5). This command (*hupakouō*) is exactly the same as in verse 1 where the children are instructed to obey their parents. The verb means to hear with submission and so to do what one is told. Those who command their obedience are their masters "according to the flesh": that is, as part of the slave-owner's natural family or household.

The command is expanded in four accompanying clauses that describe more fully the nature of the obedience. (1) "Not with eye-service, as men-pleasers" means that the slaves don't do their work just when the masters are looking. (2) "As bondservants of Christ, doing the will of God from the heart" means that the Christian slaves must regard their service to their human masters as service to Christ—for one reason, because this is Christ's command. Therefore they must obey from the heart (and not just externally), as something God Himself wills for them. (3) "With goodwill doing service, as to the Lord, and not to men" repeats the idea that what they do for their masters is in fact service to the Lord Himself (probably meaning the Lord Jesus), and so they should obey and demonstrate good will toward their masters. (4) Verse 8 means that, since they are actually serving the Lord when serving their masters, they can expect to receive appropriate reward from the Lord—which will be true whether rewarded by their masters or not.

Interestingly, *service* is a key concept here: not with eye-*service* (verse 6), as *servants* (verse 6), *doing service* (verse 7)—a verb and two nouns all built on the same Greek root for slavery. Only people who are humble and meek, thus being submissive (living in fear), are willing to make serving the central focus of their lives.

In other words, Christian slaves are to obey their masters willingly and heartily, recognizing that in serving their masters they are serving their eternal Master, the Lord Himself. The parallel passage in Colossians 3:22-24 is a little briefer but says essentially the same things.

Titus 2:9-10, also addressed to slaves, adds a few elements of similar importance. They must not be guilty of "answering back" to their masters and must not "pilfer" their master's goods. By being obedient and giving their masters good and faithful service they will "adorn the doctrine of God." In other words, their submissiveness, manifested toward their masters, will beautify the teaching of Christians about God and salvation in Jesus Christ.

We have already, in chapter 3, looked closely at 1 Peter 2:18-25. There slaves are instructed to manifest submissiveness to their masters *with all fear* (submissiveness, respectful obedience). Furthermore, this duty applies to them whether their masters are good and gentle or harsh.

2. Paul addresses the masters second, in verse 9

> ⁹ And you, masters, do the same things to them, giving up threatening, knowing that your own Master also is in heaven, and there is no partiality with Him.

The fact that Paul addresses masters directly, both in Ephesians and in Colossians, seems likely to indicate that he intends this for *Christian* masters—like Philemon, whom Paul wrote in behalf of a runaway slave named Onesimus. Masters are not addressed in the passages in Titus or 1 Peter. That he addresses them more briefly (as he did the parents in comparison with the children) probably reflects where the greater need for instruction lay. It may also result, in part, from the fact that there were fewer slave-owners than slaves in the early Christian fellowships.

There are three instructions for the masters. The first is, "Do the same things to them." This apparently means that the masters should have the same deeper understanding of their obligation that the slaves were to have (verses 5-8), which included a keen consciousness that the Lord is very much involved in the relationship. In other words, the (Christian) masters must be aware that the command of God lies behind Paul's instruction, that in their treatment of their slaves they are serving God and should do His will, and that they too can expect a reward from God.

The second instruction is "giving up threatening." The point is that they will not use threats or intimidation as a means of getting obedience from their slaves. It seems likely that this means they will not use physical punishment and the threat of it as a way of ensuring obedience.

Third, they must know that their "own Master also is in Heaven, and there is no partiality with Him." Their slaves are not the only ones obligated to a master; they, too, live under a master who has an absolute right to direct their lives. That master is God above, and He shows no partiality. He is no respecter of persons, in other words, and both slaves and masters alike are answerable to Him. The masters will get no special treatment from God.

The parallel passage in Colossians 4:1 also emphasizes that the masters have their own Master in Heaven, who directs them and to whom they must give account. There Paul adds one small but large admonition, to give their slaves "what is just and fair."

As I have said about husbands and parents (in the previous chapter), then, masters are also, in a very real sense, in subjection to their slaves. "Do the same things to them" probably reflects this. The masters are under obligation to the slaves and must subject their power over them in a way that respects their slaves and seeks their best interests. That, too, is submissiveness in practice.

Submissive Christians in the Workplace

One does not have to distill principles from the slave-master relationship to find some biblical teaching that applies to Christians on the job. Indeed, the Bible has much to say about work, even though I will not take space here to develop a biblical philosophy of work. Still, one's work is a fundamental aspect of existence, essential in defining the meaning of life. Consequently, there is a clear biblical philosophy and I will merely outline it briefly.

Even before the Fall, Adam and Eve had the responsibility to "tend and keep" the garden in which their Creator placed them (Genesis 2:15). Following their sin, the curse included the necessity of labor, now made more difficult (Genesis 3:17-19, 23). The Ten Commandments included provision for work on six days of the week (Exodus 20:9). From earliest biblical history, then, God has provided for work to be an essential part of the meaning of life. Indeed, Christian teaching based on the Bible regards one's work as a divine calling ("vocation").

The Bible has nothing good to say about those who are too lazy to work. For that matter, even compassionate Christians are not to feed such persons (2 Thessalonians 3:10; all of verses 3-12 is instructive). God-fearing people (people who are submissive before God) are expected to work to provide for their own basic needs and the needs of those for whom they are responsible (1 Thessalonians 4:11-12; 1 Timothy 5:8).

More than that, the Bible tells us that one motivation for working and earning, as Christians, is that we should have something to share with others who are in need (Ephesians 4:28). This is the kind of motive that only submissive Christians can fully exercise.

There is a biblical basis for work, then, and in all the teaching about work we can find principles to apply in our lives. This includes the passages about slaves and masters, surveyed above. Not everything there will directly convert into teaching about employees and their employers, but some basic application is clear enough.

1. Submissiveness should characterize Christians in the workplace, whether employees or employers. This takes many forms, and some of them can be broadly applied. One thing it means is that the workers submit their own personal desires to the demands of their work. The structure of the workplace, like that of government, is another manifestation of the order that God has imposed on life.

There's an old saying that "The boss may not always be right, but he's always the boss." That could be too crassly applied, of course, but the principle is sound. Often, work means obeying the boss. And if we can apply what Paul says to slaves about good and bad masters, then this may imply that we obey both reasonable and unreasonable bosses. Unlike living under governing authorities or slave-owners, however, the employee is always free to seek other employment if conditions become intolerable. And in situations in our culture there are usually some provisions for seeking change in workplace conditions in a respectful manner.

2. As in all three pairs of relationships in Ephesians, Christian employers are as much under this obligation as employees. Again, submission is involved and means that employers submit their own selfish motivations to considerations about the welfare of their employees. A Christian boss will be genuinely committed

to providing for his or her employees a full reward for their labor. While the *form* of an employer's submissiveness may be different from that of an employee, the *substance* is the same.

3. "A good day's work for a good day's pay" is another common expression that applies. A Christian employee ought to be conscientious to perform well what he or she is employed to perform. Paul warned slaves against "pilfering" their masters' goods, and there is more than one way to steal from others. Practicing the Christian faith as a laborer will include giving the full measure of time and effort that the job requires. This will include not being "clock-watchers," to use a phrase that is better understood today than the "eye-service" Paul spoke of.

4. Both Christian employees and employers ought to pursue their work "as unto the Lord." They will serve each other and fellow workers with awareness that in doing so they are serving their Lord. Employees may not be slaves, and employers may be in charge, but all of us have the Lord as our master and whatever we do should be service to Him. Colossians 3:23 applies: "Whatever you do, do it heartily, as to the Lord and not to men." This, too, is part of what Christian submissiveness means.

5. Employees and employers, alike, should go about their day-to-day activities, on the job, with a heartfelt sense of serving each other. Surely it is important that twice, in the instructions to slaves, Paul mentions their *heart*: "In sincerity of heart" (verse 5) and "from the heart" (verse 6)—even though the second phrase is, literally, "from the *soul*." What this means is that our service must be genuinely in the interests of those we serve and must come from our true selves within.

6. Indeed, *service* is the right word for Christians in the workplace, regardless of their position or status. Service only works for those who, with lowly mind and a spirit of meekness, go about their daily lives in fear or submissiveness, the very spirit of Christ. What biblically submissive Christians at work do is ask themselves, How can I serve? Even leadership should be *servant* leadership!

Conclusion

The principles outlined in this study will serve us well and can affect how we conduct ourselves in nearly all aspects of our lives, including the workplace. What Paul said to some deadbeats at Thessalonica seems a good piece of instruction to wind up this discussion: "We urge you, brethren, … that you also aspire to lead a quiet life, to mind your own business, and to work with your own hands, as we commanded you, that you may walk properly toward those who are outside, and that you may lack nothing" (1 Thessalonians 4:11-12).

I suspect that this "quiet life" matches what Peter said about "passing the time of your stay here in fear": in other words, in the humility and meekness that add up to submissiveness.

Questions and suggestions for thought or discussion

- Do you think it is appropriate to borrow principles from what Paul said to slaves and masters and apply them to the workplace situation? Why or why not?
- Identify specific ways that employees who are Christians ought to manifest submissiveness at work.

- Do the same for Christian employers or supervisors.
- Make a written or mental list of situations at your job where you find it difficult to be submissive and decide how you ought to respond. Then make up your mind to respond that way the next time you go to work.
- If there is a supervisor or situation in the workplace that is unfair, how should you go about seeking change; meanwhile, how can you show submissiveness to someone who is treating you unfairly?
- If you're an employer of others, what sort of concerns should you have for those who work under you?
- If you think of ways you ought to change your behavior where you work, in order to demonstrate that you are a Christian and appropriately submissive, ask God to help you and resolve to do things differently.
- How can we do our work as unto the Lord?

Chapter 11

Biblical Examples of Submissiveness

There are biblical examples of submissiveness, even when the word itself is not used. Recognizing and studying them can help us flesh out the concepts and words treated in this book. I have selected four, two from the Old Testament and two from the New.

Moses

In Moses's case, the word *humble* or *meek* definitely is applied to him in the record. Numbers 12:3 says, parenthetically, "Now the man Moses was very humble (KJV: meek), more than all men who were on the face of the earth." Parenthetic or not, this is inserted in a context. Moses's sister and brother, Miriam and Aaron, were speaking out against him. Their excuse was his marriage to an Ethiopian woman, but their words revealed a deeper motive.

They said, "Has the Lord indeed spoken only through Moses? Has He not spoken through us also?" Resentment and jealousy lurked in their hearts behind their speech.

Apparently Moses did not resist their agitation, but verse 2 observes, pointedly, that the Lord heard what they were saying. And the Lord, in His righteousness, called them on the carpet—as we might say. He demanded a meeting with the three of them in the tabernacle and appeared in person in a cloud, speaking up for Moses who would not defend himself and striking Miriam (perhaps she was the instigator?) with leprosy. And when Aaron pleaded with his brother, Moses prayed for Miriam (verse 13). That was submissiveness in action.

Perhaps Moses was not *always* so submissive. Raised by a Pharaoh's daughter, he was treated like royalty and could expect access to "the treasures in Egypt" (Hebrews 11:26). Even when, at 40, he began to realize that he should identify with the Israelites and be an instrument of their freedom, he asserted himself to kill an Egyptian who was apparently about to kill one of the Israelites. He took this action on his own, "supposing that his brethren would have understood that God would deliver them by his hand" (Acts 7:25). Apparently he was not meek then, and he fled the land, going to Midian where he hid out on the backside of the desert shepherding the flock of his new father-in-law (Exodus 3:1).

Perhaps it was there, during forty years of obscurity, that he learned meekness. God has a way of testing and teaching those who serve Him. At any rate, when Moses returned to Egypt and became the leader of the Israelites, he most certainly manifested a submissive spirit. As the inspired writer of Hebrews (11:26) expressed it, he was "esteeming the reproach of Christ greater riches than the treasures in Egypt." No one deliberately takes reproach on himself who is not humble and meek.

From that point on he submitted himself to do exactly what God asked of him. The people he was leading to freedom resisted him at almost every step along the way. They said, in effect, "Did you bring us out here in the wilderness to die because there were no places to bury us in Egypt? We told you then that it was better to serve the Egyptians than to die out here in the desert" (compare Exodus 14:11-12). When they got thirsty they "complained against Moses, saying 'What shall we drink?'" (Exodus 15:24). When they were hungry they said, in effect, "We wish we had died in Egypt; at least we'd have died well fed" (compare Exodus 16:3). Not long after, thirsty again, they complained, as though to say, "Why did you bring us out here to kill us and our livestock and our children with thirst?" (compare Exodus 17:3).

It was like that all the way, and worse, but Moses patiently and submissively gave them God's leadership. He did not revile them back. Once even the Lord decided He had had enough of their sin and told Moses to step aside so He could wipe them out and start over with Moses! (See Exodus 32:10.) Had there been an ounce of pride in him, he'd have accepted the offer. But Moses meekly (and boldly) interceded on the people's behalf, persuading God to relent and spare the faithless Israelites (Exodus 32:30–33:14).

Yes, near the end Moses lost it once, as told in Numbers 20. The people were complaining yet again about the lack of water. What they said this time was especially rebellious and hurtful (verses 3-5). Once more he sought the Lord, who appeared and instructed him, in effect: "Speak to the rock as the people watch, and you will give them water" (compare verse 8). But Moses was angry and self-assertive. First he angrily reviled the people, "Hear now, you rebels! Must *we* bring water for you out of this rock?" The *we* is revealing. And then he struck the rock with his rod (verses 10-11). This was not submissiveness, it was self-will. It was failure to "hallow" God before Israel (verse 12), and God punished him with a severe sentence: he could not enter Canaan with the people.

Perhaps the exception proved the rule. All in all, Moses was a humble, submissive leader, serving God and the Israelites faithfully in the face of many hardships and wicked resistance. I think we learn a lot about submissiveness from his example.

He obeyed God.

He was patient with the people.

He didn't retaliate—not against Miriam and Aaron, not against the people's complaints.

He prayed for those he led.

He stayed with what God gave him to do, serving to the end, even in the severe disappointment that came from his own failure.

Probably the reader can think of other ways Moses demonstrated submissiveness.

Joseph

How could anyone illustrate submissiveness without thinking of Joseph? The Bible doesn't use any of the key words involved in this trait, as far as I can recall, but his actions certainly demonstrated humility and meekness, that he passed the "time of his stay here in fear."

Perhaps not at first. After all, he was his father's pet, the only one of the siblings with a coat of many colors (Genesis 37:2-3). Some would say that his bold telling of the dreams that pointed to a future position of power for him indicated a foolish and self-centered indifference (Genesis 37:5-11). That may be true, although I wonder if his actions were more from an eager, naive innocence.

Whatever the case with that, Joseph's life soon turned ugly. His brothers, barely avoiding killing him, sold him as a slave and he wound up in Egypt to do Potiphar's bidding. He could have bowed up and rebelled against the unjust treatment, but instead he *served* (there's that word again!) Potiphar faithfully and—as Ephesians 6:5 says to slaves—"with fear and trembling, in sincerity of heart." In doing that, he excelled, and Potiphar realized what a jewel he had and gave him more and more authority in his house (Genesis 39:9).

Enter Potiphar's amorous wife. She relentlessly pursued Joseph. What red-blooded young man would have resisted her advances? Yet that's exactly what Joseph did, following Paul's advice exactly: he *fled* (2 Timothy 2:22). Even in his refusal to sin there was submissiveness: to God, to his master, to the greater honor and duty and purity.

And Joseph's history repeated itself. Only now, instead of his brothers, it was the woman's lies that brought about his imprisonment. In the face of severe injustice, Joseph was submissive. In the prison he served (Genesis 39:17-20). And as before he was given responsibility (verse 22). To the Pharaoh's baker and butler he showed kindness, interpreting their dreams, serving again. But the butler forgot about Joseph, who spent two more years in his unjust confinement (Genesis 40). Even so, he did not become bitter or resentful. People who are submissive don't tend to bitterness and resentment, since those emotions are signs of self-absorption.

And so it was that when the opportunity finally came, Joseph served as he had always served, interpreting Pharaoh's dream and suggesting a good management plan (Genesis 41). At last he ascended to great power, managing both the fruitful and the famine years, second in command to Egypt's supreme ruler. And the brothers came, and Joseph did not retaliate or treat them harshly. He tested them, to be sure, but when the time came to make himself known to them he provided for them and for the entire family (Genesis 42–46).

At least one more crucial thing must be noted. After their father died, the brothers were certain Joseph would seek some sort of revenge. Aware of their fear, he reassured them by saying, in essence: "Don't be afraid. Am I in the place of God? You meant evil against me, but God meant it all for good. Don't be afraid. I'll provide for you and your children." And the Bible says that he "comforted them and spoke kindly to them" (compare Genesis 50:19-21). It would be difficult to find a better example of submissiveness.

People who are proud do not serve. They do not submit to God's lordship over them, much less anyone else's, especially when facing unjustified difficulties. They do not turn down opportunities to indulge fleshly appetite. They are not faithful to duty and work or to responsibility entrusted to them. They do not resist the urge to take revenge on those who have wronged them. They do not recognize how God works in adversity.

Submissive people—those who are humble and meek and so spend the time of their stay here in fear—do all those things.

Mary, the Mother of Jesus

When I started thinking of biblical examples of submissiveness, Mary was one of the first to come to mind. The main part of her story is in Luke 1. We don't know a great deal about her before she appears on the scene there. She lived in Nazareth in "Galilee of the Gentiles," as the region was often called. She was Jewish, of the lineage of David and the tribe of Judah, but under Roman dominion such royal lineage meant next to nothing. She was a virgin, and she had been betrothed—committed for marriage by her parents—to a man named Joseph. That's about it. We don't even know how old she was, probably a teenager.

Out of the blue (!) she was visited by an angel. Naturally, she was afraid, maybe terrified. But the angel reassured her and gave her the stunning news. She would conceive and bear a son who would be Immanuel, God with us, the long-awaited Messiah Himself!

She had an obvious question. How could such a thing possibly be, seeing she was not yet married and was certainly not about to commit sin? It may be that the angel's answer was even more puzzling to her than it is to us, but at least one thing was clear: this would be the work of God Himself.

What did Mary think? What went through her mind? Did she connect this startling information with the standard Jewish expectation of a Messiah? I have an idea she did. Did she understand what the angel meant by "The Holy Spirit will come upon you, and the power of the Highest will overshadow you"? I doubt it, although I suspect it was clear that God would be the one to ignite life within her. How He could do that would have been beyond her grasp. I can only imagine the huge mixture of emotions that must have roiled deep within her.

Did she have any awareness of the consequences of a pregnancy begun without the benefit of marriage? Of what her betrothed would do? Of what other people would say? Even as late as the twentieth century some would say that she had succumbed to the advances of a blond Roman soldier stationed nearby; what then would those in her own time and community believe? They most certainly would not believe she was still a virgin. Even Joseph, as kind-hearted as he was, decided he must divorce her (Matthew 1:19).

Perhaps she didn't have time, right then, to think about such things. Her mind must have been in a whirl. But the one thing that is clearest is what she said: "Behold the maidservant of the Lord! Let it be to me according to your word" (Luke 1:38). If this was God's work, only one response was possible: submission. In her obvious humility she did not think herself too good for the reproach that would come her way, or for the shunning. In meekness she submitted to the will of God. By the way, that word she used of herself—maidservant or handmaiden—that's the feminine form of the word *doulos*, a bond-slave.

Nor was that the end of it for her. From then on she found herself willingly in submission to the hand of God in her life and in her Son's life. When she and Joseph took Him to Jerusalem at age twelve, He caused them anxiety by staying behind. She accepted that as His Father's business, even though she did not understand (Luke 2:41-50). When it seemed Jesus was unreasonable, she and her other sons went to talk with Him, and He being informed of their presence said that His disciples were His mother and brothers (Matthew 12:46-50). She did not understand that, either, but submitted to it as what His calling from God required. Even when His enemies succeeded in having Him crucified, she submitted to the pain and knelt there beneath the cross without resisting God (John 19:25-27). From the first, she had been told that a sword would pierce her heart (Luke 2:33-35), and she had submitted to whatever God had in store for her.

That's what submissive people do.

By the way, everything said here would apply to Mary's husband, Joseph, equally well. He would make another good study in submissiveness.

Barnabas

We first meet this man at the end of Acts chapter four, in connection with a description of life within the early Christian fellowship in Jerusalem. Several characteristics of that community appear: their selfless sharing with one another, the powerful witness of the apostles among them, and great grace shed on them by the God of all grace (verses 32-33). And then another aspect of their *koinonia* gets attention: they met one another's needs (verse 34).

If anyone had a need, others came to the rescue, even selling their own land or houses to be able to help (verse 35).

And Barnabas was one of those (verses 36-37). Barnabas wasn't even the name his parents gave him; that was Joses or Joseph. But the apostles named him *Barnabas,* which means "son of encouragement." Barnabas was such an encourager of others that he became known by that name. Submissive people encourage and build up others rather than promote themselves.

That wasn't all. He also, like some others, owned a piece of land and sold it and brought the money to the apostles to use it in ministering to the needs of some who were destitute. Self-promoting people don't do that. Submissive people can find it in themselves to sacrifice what they have when there is a serious need that can't be met in ordinary ways. No wonder they called him "Son of Encouragement"!

Of course we know Barnabas best for his association with Paul. There, too, he showed his submissive, selfless promotion of others. When Saul/Paul was converted after his intense persecution of the church, the Christians didn't want to risk allowing him among them. They were afraid this "conversion" was just another ploy to spy on them and have them beaten or imprisoned or executed. But Barnabas checked out Paul's story and believed in him, and he proceeded to bring Paul to the apostles and vouch for him (Acts 9:26-29). He played an important role, early, in the acceptance of Paul.

The early Christians had confidence in Barnabas. When there was a great turning to God in Antioch in Syria, the church in Jerusalem sent a man to investigate and minister; they chose Barnabas for this important mission (Acts 11:19-22). And when he arrived there and saw how richly the grace of God was being given, and how many were being converted, he felt the requirements of the work were more than he should shoulder alone and went and fetched Paul to help in the ministry (verses 23-26). A proud and self-reliant man wouldn't have done that. A submissive man was glad to involve others unselfishly.

That soon led the two men on a missionary trek, an evangelistic tour together (Acts 13-14). And it soon became clear that Paul was the more capable preacher (14:12). Almost everywhere it was Paul who got the greater attention, whether on the island of Cyprus (13:9-12) or in Pisidian Antioch (13:14-50) or in Lystra (14:8-20). It requires a humble, submissive man to let others take the spotlight and not be jealous.

Then came a parting of the ways. As they were about to set out on a second evangelistic itinerary, the question arose whether to take along a young man named John Mark who had started the first tour with them and then turned back. Paul said no. Barnabas insisted on giving him another chance. And there was sharp contention between them (Acts 15:36-41). Ever since then interpreters have argued as to whether Paul or Barnabas was right in this. I suspect they both were. When a man fails, he needs someone to hold him accountable and someone to encourage him. Regardless, Barnabas was still living out his submissive nature, giving Mark another chance to prove himself—and he did.

Submissive Christians encourage others, believe in others, promote others. That's the opposite of self-centeredness and pride. Humble, meek folks do that sort of thing. Proud, arrogant, self-assertive people don't.

- Suggest some things about the four characters used in this chapter, beyond the things already mentioned above, that show submissiveness in their lives.

- In what ways did any of these characters fail to show submissiveness? Is it possible for someone to be submissive and yet fail to act submissively in one or more circumstances? If so, why is this so?

- No doubt there are other good biblical examples of submissive believers in the Bible. Develop the story of some of them.

- For that matter, biblical examples of those who are *not* submissive can also be helpful. Their stories cast light on the nature of submissiveness by focusing on its opposite. Consider Cain. Pharaoh in Egypt. Nadab and Abihu. Balaam. King Zedekiah. Caiaphas. Pilate. Felix. Diotrephes. Pick two or three of these (or some others you think about) and describe how they did *not* display submissiveness and should have.

Chapter 12

So What Does Submissiveness Look Like?

In this concluding chapter, I want to paint a picture, drawing together the brushstrokes of the previous chapters. In those chapters I have focused on the principles, letting the biblical material guide us in understanding the nature of Christian submissiveness. The key words have been *humility* and *meekness*, and when those two are combined in a person, they lead to spending "the time of our stay here in fear"—to use the words of Peter. And that equals *submissiveness*. If you want to express this in a formula, try:

Humility + meekness = living in fear = submissiveness.

What every Christian ought to do, then, is to consider all the attitudes and behaviors of daily life and ask, "What will submissiveness look like where *I* live?" In other words, we must figure out the actual form submissiveness will take *in practice*. Earlier I referred to the difference between "form and substance." Submissiveness is the *substance* or principle; *form* refers to the practical expressions of submissiveness in one's words, thoughts, and actions.

No doubt all of us have to work that out for ourselves, one individual at a time. But everyone needs to start with the questions, and only the right questions will yield the right answers. I am therefore going to ask questions, leaving it up to each reader to come up with answers. What's important is for the answers to be in keeping with the biblical material we have surveyed in this book.

Submissiveness Before God

Do you see yourself as lowly and undeserving before Him?

Are you grateful for His mercies, His provision for your salvation, His manifold blessings, and do you express that gratitude to Him regularly? And can others tell that you are grateful to Him?

Have you accepted the salvation He offers in Jesus Christ as a gift of grace for which you have done nothing deserving? Have you given up on counting anything you can do as contributing to the reason He saves you?

Do you accept without resistance His dealings with you: where He puts you, what He gives you, what circumstances He puts you in? Another way of asking this: Do you recognize that His providential government is actively at work in all the circumstances of your life, and are you submitted to those circumstances and in them to Him?

Is God's rule fully acceptable to you? Do you yield to Him the right to run your life? In accord with that, do you accept the authority of His "rules" to live by, including the way He Himself defines the meaning of those rules? In other words, do you obey God?

When you're sure that a prompting is from God, in accord with the principles of His word, do you act on it?

Are you a disciple of Jesus Christ as the Master whom you emulate and whose teachings you follow?

Do you love and study the Bible regularly to discern the mind of God and learn to think as He thinks?

Is it necessary for you—as it was for Jesus—to be about your Father's business?

Surely submissiveness before God will require thoughtful and obedient answers to all such questions. (You may well think of some others.) God has made us and is absolute ruler of the universe. Whether we want to be or not—and as sinners, we don't want to be—we are under His lordship. It is our role to obey and serve Him with humility and meekness, yielding everything we are and have to His authority.

Disobedience and resistance, self-will and pride are opposed to being yielded or submissive before God.

Submissiveness Toward Others in General

It's one thing to think of oneself as lowly before God, but do you view yourself as lowly in relation to other people you know and interact with?

When others "wrong" you in some way, by speech or deed, how do you react? Do you retaliate? Do you feel (and show that you feel) that you deserved better than that? Do you resist, demonstrating that you aren't going to allow yourself to be mistreated in that way? Or do you accept the wrong, knowing that you are *not* too good to be wronged?

Are you quick to forgive?

Do you have a *servant's* spirit? Do others realize you're helpful? Do you give up your own convenience or resources in order to do something helpful for someone else?

How do you feel about your time? Do you guard it for yourself, or do you "spend" some of your time to do things for others, to meet needs they have, to minister to them?

The same goes for your money. Are you a generous person, willingly sharing with those in need? Indeed, what *are* you doing for the "poor and needy"—including those in need of the gospel?

How do you view yourself in comparison with others? Do you credit others with the same good motives you think you have? Are you ready to believe negative things about others that you wouldn't want to believe about yourself?

Submissiveness, like love, is a "many-splendored" thing. It reveals itself in different ways. Those who are submissive don't think themselves better than others. They don't "stand up for their rights." They are willing to forgive and restore, glad to serve, helpful, considerate, generous, self-sacrificing. No doubt you can think of other questions that help you determine whether the humility and meekness that amount to submissiveness toward others are true of you.

Selfishness comes in many forms. All of them are opposed to submissiveness.

Submissiveness to Governing Authorities

Do you recognize that human government is an institution ordained by God to serve and advance His providential government of our world?

What is your attitude toward the laws of the land? Do you obey them?

Can others tell that you respect the institutions of government, whether local, state, or national? Or do the things you say show disrespect and foster the same attitude in others who hear you?

Do you pray for those who govern us?

When you can't appreciate the ways of someone who is in authority, do you discipline yourself to maintain respect for the office that person holds? And speak of him in such a way that influences others to have respect?

Do you calculate your taxes without dishonesty and pay them without grumbling?

Knowing that you ought to obey God rather than men when the two are in conflict, do you find it too easy to categorize things you want as things God has spoken about?

The submissive Christian recognizes that those who govern us, even when they are unbelievers or act in ways unbecoming to their office, are still ministers of God to promote what is good and orderly and repress what is wicked and disorderly. Whenever we think we must disobey the authorities because they have asked us to disobey God (a very rare occurrence in our country), we must be sure of our biblical grounds.

Submissiveness in the Home

For husbands. Do you love your wife in the same way Christ loved the church and gave Himself for it? Given that *love* means choosing the other's best interests over one's own, are you sacrificing selfish interests and desires for the sake of your wife's well-being?

Is your leadership in the home *servant* leadership? If you have a decision to make, do you get your wife's input and consider her views and needs *before* you make the decision?

For wives. Do you recognize your husband's leadership responsibility in your home and gladly submit to it as a way of submitting to the authority of the Lord Himself?

Do you demonstrate your love for your husband in service?

For both. In the spirit of Philippians 2:4, do you focus on the needs of your spouse and children rather than on your own? Are they empowered by the time and energy you devote to them?

For parents. Do your children ever see that you sacrifice your own interests on their behalf? Are you serving them by being fully considerate of their needs?

Are you giving your children the loving discipline and instruction that will direct them aright, in the ways of the Lord? Does your teaching of them reflect both the words you use and an example that is consistent with those words?

For children. Do you honor your parents by submitting to their authority and doing so both inwardly and outwardly?

Do you deliberately try to learn from them so that you will not have to make mistakes that you will experience as costly?

If you're grown, and perhaps have a family of your own, do you honor your parents by supporting and providing for them as needed? And continuing to show them the respect that the Lord asks you to show?

I have no doubt that you can think of many more questions, including very specific ones that will probe the nature of submissiveness within family relationships. Probably in this set of relationships more than any other (except for submission toward God) submissiveness is of crucial importance. Every member of the family needs to be humble and meek and to act in accord with that attitude. Self-sacrifice and service will be hallmarks of that grace. Living that way will incorporate a keen awareness of the needs of one's spouse, children, and parents, and that awareness will lead to action toward meeting those needs.

Submissiveness at Work

For employees. Do you appreciate your job, both for its own value as a way of life that is good for you and pleasing to God, and for its value in enabling you to provide for yourself and your family? And do you also see in your work a means of earning something you can share with others in need?

Do you give a good day's work for a good day's pay, when both are measured in the terms by which your responsibilities and remuneration were defined when you took the job?

Do you set a good example for other employees, showing faithfulness, integrity, and a cooperative spirit, genuinely devoting yourself to the welfare and success of the organization you work for?

Do you demonstrate, by word and attitude, a proper respect for those who are in authority over you where you are employed?

If you see the need for corrections or improvements in your workplace, do you work for improvement within channels—a defined "chain of command," for example—and demonstrate a healthy and constructive attitude?

For employers or managers. Do you give serious consideration to the fact that you yourself are employed in the service of God? And then allow that awareness to affect how you relate to your employees?

Are you genuinely committed to providing a good day's pay for a good day's work, with appropriate benefits—at a level that matches careful consideration of what employees need to "make a living"?

Do you take steps appropriate for ensuring the welfare of your employees, especially at work but also in regard to the "living" that their work for you ought to provide? Do you sacrifice selfish motivations in order to serve those who work for you?

Submissiveness can be tested on the job, for sure. Christians are responsible to strengthen their own witness by being good employees and serving just as faithfully as they would if the business were theirs. They should rejoice when the company makes a prof-it—and the company should share its profits with the employees.

Submissiveness in the Body of Christ

The church is the body of Christ, which includes all true Christians of all times and places. The local church, specifically, is a "visible" microcosm of the body of Christ within a given community.

Are you committed to the spiritual welfare of every person in your church? So much so that you will do what you can, in whatever role you play, to serve and edify them?

When discipline is needed by others, are you available to work with them to restore them (in the spirit of Galatians 6:1)?

If the church believes *you* need the discipline, do you submit to its processes that are aimed toward your correction and restoration?

Do you recognize and respect the leadership roles of those who are chosen by the church to be in office, including the pastor (or pastors) and deacons? Do you honor them for the office they hold and do your part to promote their honor by others? Do you submit to their leadership so long as they lead within the parameters set by the church?

Do you serve others and sacrifice your own selfish concerns for the sake of the spiritual health and up-building of the church as a whole? Do you give generously of your time and money toward this end? Do you faithfully attend and *participate* in the public worship services?

If you're a pastor or have other leadership responsibilities, is yours a *servant* leadership? In other words, are you sacrificing self-centered interests—time, money, energy—on behalf of the needs of those you're ministering to?

Along with the family and human government, the church—especially but not exclusively the local church—is one of the organizations instituted by God for the service of the human race in general and His people in particular. Submissiveness should characterize every member of the church, and it ought to take the form of orderly service to promote its health and growth as a community of believers devoted to each other.

Questions for Leaders, Including Pastors

While my primary focus in this work is on all believers in everyday Christian living, the leaders must not be left out—especially leaders of Christian organizations and local churches.

Are you a *servant*-leader?

As a leader, before you make decisions that affect those whom you lead, do you seek their input, their concerns and suggestions? Do you keep them informed?

As a pastor, do you act and lead within the framework of the governmental structure adopted by your church. If your church professes to practice *congregational* church government *within the local church*, do you make arbitrary decisions about the life of the church, or do you provide reasons for your recommendations and let the church decide? And then accept their decisions humbly?

Are you so committed to the spiritual well-being of your flock that you spend the necessary time in study and prayer and personal interaction to foster effectively their spiritual maturing?

Are you so committed to the increase of your church that you sacrifice time and energy to target and work toward the conversion of people outside the church?

Does your church recognize that you are self-sacrificing rather than self-asserting?

There are many philosophies of leadership in the marketplace. For that matter, there may be different approaches that will work well. But the only *basic* approach to leadership that is right for the church and church-related organizations is the model taught by Jesus Christ and exemplified and elaborated in the New Testament. That model begins with Jesus' words in Luke 22:25-26: "The kings of the Gentiles exercise lordship over them, and those who exercise authority over them are called benefactors. But not so among you; on the contrary, he who is greatest among you, let him be as the younger, and he who governs as he who serves." Mark 10:42-45 says the same thing in somewhat different words: "Whoever desires to become great among you shall be your servant." Whatever your leadership role is, and whatever structure you build, build it on this foundation.

If you do, you will lead as one who is submissive, as a self-sacrificing servant of those you lead.

Conclusion: Some Suggestions About Developing Submissiveness

Submissiveness, including its primary elements of humility and meekness, is the fruit of the Spirit. It is a supernatural work. But there are enough commands about this grace that we cannot escape responsibility to cooperate with the Spirit in the production of this fruit in our lives.

Here are some not-so-easy, practical suggestions about developing this fruit in your life. And, by the way, they can be used for developing *any* of the spiritual graces.

First, whether using this book or your own independent study, flesh out a fuller picture of what the Bible means by submissiveness, including the humility and meekness that are its essential components. There is a lot of biblical material on this subject, and this is what I've tried to explore in this volume.

Second, pray to God for this grace. Remember, this is the fruit of the Spirit, so make this a matter of continuing prayer. Ask God to produce humility and meekness—submissiveness—in your life.

Third, make a list of all the ways you can think of that this grace would be manifested in your daily life if you had it. Don't let yourself off the hook, here. Think carefully about all your relationships and ask yourself, If I were submissive, if I were humble and meek, how would that affect me in these relationships? What would this look like in my words and conduct? Be very specific and express this in specific ways, large or small, that would be a part of your relationships.

Fourth, pray again: namely, that the Spirit of God will help you act and speak in the exact ways you have listed.

Fifth, then go act and speak in those very ways—whether you "feel" like it or not. I expect someone will say this is just good psychology, that if you act in a certain way enough you'll come to feel that way. Maybe that's true to some degree, but it's not what I'm saying. What I'm saying is that acting and speaking as you truly understand submissiveness would act and speak is *obedience.* It's the way you *obey* all those commands to be humble, to be meek, to be in subjection.

And if you figure out what this grace looks like in practice, and sincerely ask God to help you be that way, and then do what you figured out it looks like, you'll find the grace of submissiveness is a ripening fruit in your life.

And that will be for your joy and for the glory of your Savior who is changing you into His likeness by the work of His Spirit (2 Corinthians 3:17-18).